Philosophical Foundation of Education

Philosophical Foundation of Education

Premchand Jogi

CRESCENT
PUBLISHING CORPORATION

Philosophical Foundation of Education

Edition 2026

ISBN 978-81-8342-127-0

Published by
CRESCENT PUBLISHING CORPORATION
4806/24, Mathur Lane,
Ansari Road, Darya Ganj,
New Delhi - 110 002
Ph.: 011 - 23244131
Mob.: + 91 - 9711991838, 9999021668
E-mail: crescentbook@gmail.com
Website: www.crescentpublishingcorp.weebly.com

Printed at:
Balaji Digital
Delhi

Preface

Through history, education has been viewed as an optimistic endeavour by most societies, bringing in such multifaceted objectives likes equipping people with the skills to produce goods and services, to respond creativity and effectively to the world they live, satiate their curiosity, stretch their abilities to their best and satisfy their aesthetic impulses. To achieve these objectives people need to acquire reliable knowledge and to think systematically. Today, as the definitions of educations are constantly redefined, educations are constantly redefined education has become crucial not only in terms of development and progress, but also in philosophy and other areas of thought.

The philosophy of education has had a long history, even as it is being continuously build and rebuild in contemporary times. Over the course of human history education has appeared in may forms, both formalised and informal. However, no matter what the social context, the philosophies which led to these schools of education, they form the foundations for much of our present ways of dealing with education. This book takes a pragmatic approach to delineating the philosophical foundations of education enumerating upon the thoughts of major philosophies in this field, and contextualising them within their contemporary needs and times. In addition, it assesses these foundations, reviewing their impact the world over. Further, it also takes a look at current situations and their constitution and deconstruction of these educational philosophies.

We hope that the erudition and insight of the book prove satisfactory to the readers.

Premchand Jogi

Contents

1

Curriculum Theories

Outcome-based Learning

In outcome-based learning, all school programmes and instructional efforts are designed to have produced specific, lasting results in students by the time they leave school.

One of the leading examples of an outcome-based learning programme is the Outcome-Driven Developmental Model (ODDM) of the school system in Johnson City, New York. The principles followed by outcome-based learning practitioners include:

— *Clarity of focus* around significant, culminating exit outcomes, which are defined by each school

— *Expansion of available time and resources* so that all students successfully reach the exit outcomes

— *Consistent, high expectations* of 100% success

— *Explicit relationships* between any learning experience and the ultimate outcomes to which that experience is essential

Core Curriculum

In a c :e curriculum, a predetermined body of skills, know .dge, and abilities is taught to all students.

The core curriculum movement assumes there is an uniform body of knowledge that all students should know. Presumably, this curriculum will produce educated and responsible graduates for the community. Unfortunately, there often isn't much consensus on who is the community and who speaks for the community. In fact, there is a growing conflict about what topics a core curriculum should contain. Some advocates would limit the core to basic academic subjects like English, math, science, and government, while others would include general learner outcomes such as problem solving, critical thinking, teamwork, and community service.

Curriculum affects the Following Elements of Education:

— *Curriculum*—The curriculum is built on a mandated core, which is defined and designed outside the classroom. All students learn a common set of knowledge, skills, and abilities. Though academic content remains the primary focus of the core curriculum, some core teaching is moving toward application and problem solving.

— *Instruction*—Instruction is based on a defined core content. Rather than focusing on discovery, teaching revolves around imparting a predetermined body of knowledge. Although the core curriculum method does not preclude using critical thinking, problem solving, and team learning, it prompts teaching toward the "correct" answer.

— *Assessment*—The core content literally shapes the assessment process. The core curriculum method easily lends itself to traditional testing based on information recall, as well as the use of conventional letter grades. However, a core curriculum doesn't preclude the use of authentic assessment and portfolios.

Whole Language

This philosophy about curriculum—in both language arts and a broader, more general programme—is based on recent research of how children acquire oral and written language skills.

Basic Elements

Because knowledge doesn't exist separately from the people who construct it, whole language practitioners don't see curriculum as a prescribed course of study or a particular set of instructional materials. Instead, they see it as the cognitive experience each learner has. Whole language doesn't just include the specific content being thought about, it also includes how a student "demonstrates" a particular task, as well as what he or she expects from a language learning situation.

The fundamental concern of someone who uses language is making sense. To a learner, reading and writing are crucial to forming an understanding of the world. A whole language curriculum treats the learner as a legitimate conversation partner and someone who seeks meaning. Therefore, whole language practitioners support their students' efforts—even those that aren't entirely accurate—rather than directing their thinking and language use.

We learn language cumulatively by using it. Each language encounter, whether oral or written, builds more knowledge about the world, the function of symbols, and communication strategies. Consequently, each language transaction helps us perform the next one, whether it be oral, written, or mental. A whole language curriculum immerses students in situations requiring open-ended, complex language use.

The teacher's role in such a curriculum is one of "interpretive" teaching, or "kidwatching"—in other words, making sense of how students engage in language learning and offering experiences that support their experiments.

Language learning is a social activity; it requires negotiating meaning and taking in feedback from partners. Whole language practitioners work to provoke, elicit, and show interest in communication exchanges—both learner-learner and learner-teacher.

With language learning, there is always the risk of trying new strategies, and error is inherent in the process. Practitioners encourage this spirit by reading meaning into children's speech or writing attempts, and by "hearing and seeing through" errors and spelling inventions, rather than correcting and prescribing exactness. With the support of their teachers, the children's spoken and written experiments help them locate and learn the conventional language usage.

Character Education

This curriculum method revolves around developing "good character" in students by practicing and teaching moral values and decision making.

Character education assumes that schools don't just have the responsibility to help students get "smart," they also have the responsibility to help them cultivate basic moral values to guide their behaviour throughout life.

Today's emphasis on character education is propelled by the decline in family influence, downward trends in youth character, and the emerging consensus of shared ethical values.

Character education teaches students to understand, commit to, and act on shared ethical values—in other words, "know the good, desire the good, and do the good." Typical core values include respect, responsibility, trustworthiness, fairness, caring, and community participation.

Schools committed to character education tend to:

— Emphasize the importance of adults modelling values in the classroom as well as in their everyday interactions

— Help students clarify their values and build personal bonds and responsibilities to one another

— Use the traditional curriculum as a vehicle for teaching values and examining moral questions

— Encourage moral reflection through debate, journals, and discussion

— Encourage values in action through community service and other community involvement strategies

— Support teacher development and dialogue among educators on the moral dimension of their job

The influence of character education is evident in the outcomes of many school districts emphasizing qualities such as "participant in a democratic society," "contributor to the community," and "ethical global citizen."

Multiculturalism

Multiculturalism is based on the belief that varying cultural dynamics are the fourth force—along with the psychodynamic, behavioural, and humanistic forces—explaining human behaviour. Since the ability to recognize our own and others' cultural lenses is essential to all learning, it must be taught, along with communication and thinking skills, as prerequisites to learning.

The National Council for Social Studies, in its *Curriculum Guidelines for Multicultural Education,* lists the key functions of multicultural education as:

— Providing students with a sharp sense of self
— Helping students understand the experience of ethnic and cultural groups in history
— Helping students understand that conflict between ideals and reality exist in every human society
— Helping students develop decision-making, social participation, and citizenship skills
— Achieving full literacy in at least two languages

"Multicultural" is broadly understood to include experiences shaping perceptions common to age, gender, religion, socio-economic status, and exceptionality of any kind, as well as cultural, linguistic, and racial identities.

This controversial approach has stirred passionate critics, who contend that it aims to replace "Eurocentrism" with "othercentrisms." Critics also allege that multiculturalism hinders the assimilation of various cultures into America's greatest hallmark: the melting pot.

Tech Prep

Tech prep is most traditionally and frequently defined as a four-year programme (during grades 11-14) that leads to an associate degree or two-year certificate in a specific career field. This curriculum includes a common core of required mathematics, science communications, and technologies that is integrated, applied, and sequenced.

There is a strong consensus that American schools have generally ignored the average student: the middle 50% of teenagers who complete high school, but do not attend four-year colleges, universities, or graduate schools. These students are no longer prepared to enter today's changed workforce, which demands workers who can think, problem solve, work in teams, and apply knowledge. The tech prep curriculum was designed as the instructional strategy for preparing such students to work in a labour market that requires more technical skills.

Some critics question whether a tech prep curriculum significantly differs from vocational education. And others want high schools to reorganize themselves, offering students only a college prep or a tech prep course of study.

Tech Prep Curriculum affects the Following Elements of Education:

— *Curriculum*: High schools and community colleges coordinate the tech prep curriculum together, eliminating duplication and ensuring skills are acquired in the best possible sequence. Critics of tech prep programmes maintain that neither the curriculum in the high school nor the community college has changed to reflect the issues and problems of today's workplace. Predominantly, the focus is on teaching math, science, and communication for both application and contextual purposes.

— *Instruction*: Tech prep instruction is still classroom-oriented. Most of the occupational skills are taught in the laboratory setting. There is a strong push to try integrating what happens in the academic classroom with activities in the occupational labs.

— *Assessment:* In the occupational labs, we see a greater use of assessing work samples and projects than in traditional classes. However, there is still a heavy reliance on traditional tests and grades. The drawback of this is that although tech prep prepares students for the job market, it may not prepare them for the lack of traditional assessment in the workplace—in other words, employers don't rate employee performances with letter grades and test scores.

Paideia

This "essentialist" curriculum created in 1982 by Mortimer Adler and The Paideia Group proposes a single, required, 12-year course in general, humanistic learning as a foundation for the future learning of all students.

The Paideia plan is built on the understanding that education serves to prepare individuals for (1) earning a living, (2) citizenship, and (3) self-development. With that in mind, here is the plan's proposed framework:

Theodore Sizer of the Paideia Group insists that Paideia is not a detailed curriculum for deliberate reasons. The Paideia Group believes that only the teachers and principals who can change education should design a specific curriculum blueprint. Instead, the Paideia plan provides a framework and process for "crafting the critical details of the programme in ways appropriate to their own communities."

Constructivism

Constructivism is a philosophy of learning founded on the premise that, by reflecting on our experiences, we construct our own understanding of the world we live in. Each of us generates our own "rules" and "mental models," which we use to make sense of our experiences. Learning, therefore, is simply the process of adjusting our mental models to accommodate new experiences.

There are several guiding principles of constructivism:

— Learning is a search for meaning. Therefore, learning

must start with the issues around which students are actively trying to construct meaning.

— Meaning requires understanding wholes as well as parts. And parts must be understood in the context of wholes. Therefore, the learning process focuses on primary concepts, not isolated facts.

— In order to teach well, we must understand the mental models that students use to perceive the world and the assumptions they make to support those models.

— The purpose of learning is for an individual to construct his or her own meaning, not just memorize the "right" answers and regurgitate someone else's meaning. Since education is inherently interdisciplinary, the only valuable way to measure learning is to make the assessment part of the learning process, ensuring it provides students with information on the quality of their learning.

Constructivism Impacts Learning

— *Curriculum*: Constructivism calls for the elimination of a standardised curriculum. Instead, it promotes using curricula customised to the students' prior knowledge. Also, it emphasizes hands-on problem solving.

— *Instruction*: Under the theory of constructivism, educators focus on making connections between facts and fostering new understanding in students. Instructors tailor their teaching strategies to student responses and encourage students to analyse, interpret, and predict information. Teachers also rely heavily on open-ended questions and promote extensive dialogue among students.

— *Assessment*: Constructivism calls for the elimination of grades and standardised testing. Instead, assessment becomes part of the learning process so that students play a larger role in judging their own progress.

BEHAVIOURISM

Behaviourism is a theory of animal and human learning that only focuses on objectively observable behaviours and discounts mental activities. Behaviour theorists define learning as nothing more than the acquisition of new behaviour.

Experiments by behaviorists identify conditioning as a universal learning process. There are two different types of conditioning, each yielding a different behavioural pattern:

— *Classic conditioning* occurs when a natural reflex responds to a stimulus. The most popular example is Pavlov's observation that dogs salivate when they eat or even see food. Essentially, animals and people are biologically "wired" so that a certain stimulus will produce a specific response.

— *Behavioural or operant conditioning* occurs when a response to a stimulus is reinforced. Basically, operant conditioning is a simple feedback system: If a reward or reinforcement follows the response to a stimulus, then the response becomes more probable in the future. For example, leading behaviourist B.F. Skinner used reinforcement techniques to teach pigeons to dance and bowl a ball in a mini-alley.

There have been many criticisms of behaviourism, including the following:

— Behaviourism does not account for all kinds of learning, since it disregards the activities of the mind.

— Behaviourism does not explain some learning—such

as the recognition of new language patterns by young children—for which there is no reinforcement mechanism.

— Research has shown that animals adapt their reinforced patterns to new information. For instance, a rat can shift its behaviour to respond to changes in the layout of a maze it had previously mastered through reinforcements.

Behaviourism Impacts Learning

This theory is relatively simple to understand because it relies only on observable behaviour and describes several universal laws of behaviour. Its positive and negative reinforcement techniques can be very effective—both in animals, and in treatments for human disorders such as autism and antisocial behaviour. Behaviourism often is used by teachers, who reward or punish student behaviours.

Piaget

Swiss biologist and psychologist Jean Piaget is renowned for constructing a highly influential model of child development and learning. Piaget's theory is based on the idea that the developing child builds cognitive structures—in other words, mental "maps," schemes, or networked concepts for understanding and responding to physical experiences within his or her environment. Piaget further attested that a child's cognitive structure increases in sophistication with development, moving from a few innate reflexes such as crying and sucking to highly complex mental activities.

Piaget's theory identifies four developmental stages and the processes by which children progress through them. The four stages are:

— *Sensorimotor stage (birth - 2 years old)*—The child, through physical interaction with his or her environment, builds a set of concepts about reality and how it works. This is the stage where a child does not know that physical objects remain in existence even when out of sight (object permanance).

— *Preoperational stage (ages 2-7)*: The child is not yet able to conceptualize abstractly and needs concrete physical situations.

— *Concrete operations (ages 7-11)*: As physical experience accumulates, the child starts to conceptualize, creating logical structures that explain his or her physical experiences. Abstract problem solving is also possible at this stage. For example, arithmetic equations can be solved with numbers, not just with objects.

— *Formal operations (beginning at ages 11-15)*: By this point, the child's cognitive structures are like those of an adult and include conceptual reasoning.

Piaget outlined several principles for building cognitive structures. During all development stages, the child experiences his or her environment using whatever mental maps he or she has constructed so far. If the experience is a repeated one, it fits easily—or is assimilated—into the child's cognitive structure so that he or she maintains mental "equilibrium." If the experience is different or new, the child loses equilibrium, and alters his or her cognitive structure to accommodate the new conditions. This way, the child erects more and more adequate cognitive structures.

Piaget's Theory Impacts Learning

— *Curriculum*: Educators must plan a developmentally

appropriate curriculum that enhances their students' logical and conceptual growth.

— *Instruction*: Teachers must emphasize the critical role that experiences—or interactions with the surrounding environment—play in student learning. For example, instructors have to take into account the role that fundamental concepts, such as the permanence of objects, play in establishing cognitive structures.

Neuroscience

Neuroscience is the study of the human nervous system, the brain, and the biological basis of consciousness, perception, memory, and learning. The nervous system and the brain are the physical foundation of the human learning process. Neuroscience links our observations about cognitive behaviour with the actual physical processes that support such behaviour. This theory is still "young" and is undergoing rapid, controversial development.

Some of the key findings of neuroscience are:

— *The brain has a triad structure*: Our brain actually contains three brains: the lower or reptilian brain that controls basic sensory motor functions; the mammalian or limbic brain that controls emotions, memory, and biorhythms; and the neocortex or thinking brain that controls cognition, reasoning, language, and higher intelligence.

— *The brain is not a computer*: The structure of the brain's neuron connections is loose, flexible, "webbed," overlapping, and redundant. It's impossible for such a system to function like a linear or parallel-processing computer. Instead, the brain is better described as a self-organising system.

— *The brain changes with use, throughout our lifetime*: Mental concentration and effort alters the physical structure of the brain. Our nerve cells (neurons) are connected by branches called dendrites. There are about 10 billion neurons in the brain and about 1,000 trillion connections. The possible combinations of connections is about ten to the one-millionth power.

Neuroscience Impacts Education

When educators take neuroscience into account, they organise a curriculum around real experiences and integrated, "whole" ideas. Plus, they focus on instruction that promotes complex thinking and the "growth" of the brain. Neuroscience proponents advocate continued learning and intellectual development throughout adulthood.

Brain-based Learning

This learning theory is based on the structure and function of the brain. As long as the brain is not prohibited from fulfilling its normal processes, learning will occur.

People often say that everyone **can** learn. Yet the reality is that everyone **does** learn. Every person is born with a brain that functions as an immensely powerful processor. Traditional schooling, however, often inhibits learning by discouraging, ignoring, or punishing the brain's natural learning processes.

The core principles of brain-based learning state that:

— The brain is a parallel processor, meaning it can perform several activities at once, like tasting and smelling.

— Learning engages the whole physiology.

— The search for meaning is innate.

— he search for meaning comes through patterning.
— Emotions are critical to patterning.
— The brain processes wholes and parts simultaneously.
— Learning involves both focused attention and peripheral perception.
— Learning involves both conscious and unconscious processes.
— We have two types of memory: spatial and rote.
— We understand best when facts are embedded in natural, spatial memory.
— Learning is enhanced by challenge and inhibited by threat.
— Each brain is unique.

The three instructional techniques associated with brain-based learning are:

— *Orchestrated immersion*: Creating learning environments that fully immerse students in an educational experience
— *Relaxed alertness:* Trying to eliminate fear in learners, while maintaining a highly challenging environment
— *Active processing*: Allowing the learner to consolidate and internalize information by actively processing it

Brain-Based Learning Impacts Education

— *Curriculum*: Teachers must design learning around student interests and make learning contextual.
— *Instruction*: Educators let students learn in teams and use peripheral learning. Teachers structure learning around real problems, encouraging students to also learn in settings outside the classroom and the school building.

— *Assessment*: Since all students are learning, their assessment should allow them to understand their own learning styles and preferences. This way, students monitor and enhance their own learning process.

How the brain works has a significant impact on what kinds of learning activities are most effective. Educators need to help students have appropriate experiences and capitalise on those experiences. As Renate Caine illustrates on p. 113 of her book *Making Connections*, three interactive elements are essential to this process:

— Teachers must immerse learners in complex, interactive experiences that are both rich and real. One excellent example is immersing students in a foreign culture to teach them a second language. Educators must take advantage of the brain's ability to parallel process.

— Students must have a personally meaningful challenge. Such challenges stimulate a student's mind to the desired state of alertness.

— In order for a student to gain insight about a problem, there must be intensive analysis of the different ways to approach it, and about learning in general. This is what's known as the "active processing of experience."

A few other tenets of brain-based learning include:

— Feedback is best when it comes from reality, rather than from an authority figure.

— People learn best when solving realistic problems.

— The big picture can't be separated from the details.

— Because every brain is different, educators should allow learners to customise their own environments.

— The best problem solvers are those that laugh!

Designers of educational tools must be artistic in their creation of brain-friendly environments. Instructors need to realize that the best way to learn is not through lecture, but by participation in realistic environments that let learners try new things safely.

Learning Styles

This approach to learning emphasizes the fact that individuals perceive and process information in very different ways. The learning styles theory implies that how much individuals learn has more to do with whether the educational experience is geared toward their particular style of learning than whether or not they are "smart." In fact, educators should not ask, "Is this student smart?" but rather "How is this student smart?"

The concept of learning styles is rooted in the classification of psychological types. The learning styles theory is based on research demonstrating that, as the result of heredity, upbringing, and current environmental demands, different individuals have a tendency to both perceive and process information differently. The different ways of doing so are generally classified as:

— *Concrete and abstract perceivers:* Concrete perceivers absorb information through direct experience, by doing, acting, sensing, and feeling. Abstract perceivers, however, take in information through analysis, observation, and thinking.

— *Active and reflective processors:* Active processors make sense of an experience by immediately using the new information. Reflective processors make sense of an experience by reflecting on and thinking about it.

Traditional schooling tends to favour abstract perceiving and reflective processing. Other kinds of learning aren't rewarded and reflected in curriculum, instruction, and assessment nearly as much.

Learning Styles Theory Impacts Education

— *Curriculum*—Educators must place emphasis on intuition, feeling, sensing, and imagination, in addition to the traditional skills of analysis, reason, and sequential problem solving.

— *Instruction*: Teachers should design their instruction methods to connect with all four learning styles, using various combinations of experience, reflection, conceptualization, and experimentation. Instructors can introduce a wide variety of experiential elements into the classroom, such as sound, music, visuals, movement, experience, and even talking.

— *Assessment*: Teachers should employ a variety of assessment techniques, focusing on the development of "whole brain" capacity and each of the different learning styles.

MULTIPLE INTELLIGENCES

This theory of human intelligence, developed by psychologist Howard Gardner, suggests there are at least seven ways that people have of perceiving and understanding the world. Gardner labels each of these ways a distinct "intelligence"—in other words, a set of skills allowing individuals to find and resolve genuine problems they face.

Gardner defines an "intelligence" as a group of abilities that:

— Is somewhat autonomous from other human capacities

— Has a core set of information-processing operations

— Has a distinct history in the stages of development we each pass through

— Has plausible roots in evolutionary history

While Gardner suggests his list of intelligences may not be exhaustive, he identifies the following seven:

— *Verbal-Linguistic*: The ability to use words and language

— *Logical-Mathematical*: The capacity for inductive and deductive thinking and reasoning, as well as the use of numbers and the recognition of abstract patterns

— *Visual-Spatial*: The ability to visualize objects and spatial dimensions, and create internal images and pictures

— *Body-Kinesthetic*: The wisdom of the body and the ability to control physical motion

— *Musical-Rhythmic*: The ability to recognize tonal patterns and sounds, as well as a sensitivity to rhythms and beats

— *Interpersonal*; The capacity for person-to-person communications and relationships

— *Intrapersonal*: The spiritual, inner states of being, self-reflection, and awareness

Multiple Intelligences Impact Learning

— *Curriculum*: Traditional schooling heavily favors the verbal-linguistic and logical-mathematical intelligences. Gardner suggests a more balanced curriculum that incorporates the arts, self-awareness, communication, and physical education.

— *Instruction*: Gardner advocates instructional methods that appeal to all the intelligences, including role playing, musical performance, cooperative learning, reflection, visualisation, story telling, and so on.

— *Assessment*: This theory calls for assessment methods that take into account the diversity of intelligences, as well as self-assessment tools that help students understand their intelligences.

Right Brain and Left Brain

This theory of the structure and functions of the mind suggests that the two different sides of the brain control two different "modes" of thinking. It also suggests that each of us prefers one mode over the other.

Experimentation has shown that the two different sides, or hemispheres, of the brain are responsible for different manners of thinking. The following table illustrates the differences between left-brain and right-brain thinking:

Left Brain	Right Brain
Logical	Random
Sequential	Intuitive
Rational	Holistic
Analytical	Synthesizing
Objective	Subjective
Looks at parts	Looks at wholes

Most individuals have a distinct preference for one of these styles of thinking. Some, however, are more whole-brained and equally adept at both modes. In general, schools tend to favour left-brain modes of thinking, while downplaying the right-brain ones. Left-brain scholastic subjects focus on logical thinking, analysis, and accuracy. Right-brained subjects, on the other hand, focus on aesthetics, feeling, and creativity.

Right-Brain vs. Left-Brain Thinking Impacts Learning

— *Curriculum*: In order to be more "whole-brained" in

their orientation, schools need to give equal weight to the arts, creativity, and the skills of imagination and synthesis.

— *Instruction*: To foster a more whole-brained scholastic experience, teachers should use instruction techniques that connect with both sides of the brain. They can increase their classroom's right-brain learning activities by incorporating more patterning, metaphors, analogies, role playing, visuals, and movement into their reading, calculation, and analytical activities.

— *Assessment*: For a more accurate whole-brained evaluation of student learning, educators must develop new forms of assessment that honour right-brained talents and skills.

Communities of Practice

This approach views learning as an act of membership in a "community of practice." The theory seeks to understand both the structure of communities and how learning occurs in them.

Basic Elements

The communities of practice concept was pioneered by the Institute for Research on Learning, a spin-off of the Xerox Corporation in Palo Alto, CA. The Institute pursues a cross-disciplinary approach to learning research, involving cognitive scientists, organisational anthropologists, and traditional educators. Communities of practice is based on the following assumptions:

— *Learning is fundamentally a social phenomenon:* People organise their learning around the social communities to which they belong. Therefore, schools are only powerful learning environments for students whose social communities coincide with that school.

— *Knowledge is integrated in the life of communities that share values, beliefs, languages, and ways of doing things:* These are called communities of practice. Real knowledge is integrated in the doing, social relations, and expertise of these communities.

— *The processes of learning and membership in a community of practice are inseparable:* Because learning is intertwined with community membership, it is what lets us belong to and adjust our status in the group. As we change our learning, our identity—and our relationship to the group—changes.

— *Knowledge is inseparable from practice:* It is not possible to know without doing. By doing, we learn.

— *Empowerment—or the ability to contribute to a community—creates the potential for learning:* Circumstances in which we engage in real action that has consequences for both us and our community create the most powerful learning environments.

Communities of Practice Impacts Education

This approach to learning suggests teachers understand their students' communities of practice and acknowledge the learning students do in such communities. The communities of practice theory also suggests educators structure learning opportunities that embed knowledge in both work practices and social relations—for example, apprenticeships, school-based learning, service learning, and so on. Plus, educators should create opportunities for students to solve real problems with adults, in real learning situations.

Control Theory

This theory of motivation proposed by William Glasser contends that behaviour is never caused by a response to an outside stimulus. Instead, the control theory states that behaviour is inspired by what a person **wants** most at any given time: survival, love, power, freedom, or any other basic human need.

Responding to complaints that today's students are "unmotivated," Glasser attests that all living creatures "control" their behaviour to maximize their need satisfaction. According to Glasser, if students are not motivated to do their schoolwork, it's because they view schoolwork as irrelevant to their basic human needs.

— Boss teachers use rewards and punishment to coerce students to comply with rules and complete required assignments. Glasser calls this "leaning on your shovel" work. He shows how high percentages of students recognise that the work they do—even when their teachers praise them—is such low-level work.

— Lead teachers, on the other hand, avoid coercion completely. Instead, they make the intrinsic rewards of doing the work clear to their students, correlating any proposed assignments to the students' basic needs. Plus, they only use grades as temporary indicators of what has and hasn't been learned, rather than a reward. Lead teachers will "fight to protect" highly engaged, deeply motivated students who are doing quality work from having to fulfil meaningless requirements.

Control Theory Impacts Learning

— *Curriculum*: Teachers must negotiate both content and method with students. Students' basic needs literally help shape how and what they are taught.

— *Instruction*: Teachers rely on cooperative, active learning techniques that enhance the power of the learners. Lead teachers make sure that all assignments meet some degree of their students' need satisfaction. This secures student loyalty, which carries the class through whatever relatively meaningless tasks might be necessary to satisfy official requirements.

— *Assessment*: Instructors only give "good grades"—those that certify quality work—to satisfy students' need for power. Courses for which a student doesn't earn a "good grade" are not recorded on that student's transcript. Teachers grade students using an absolute standard, rather than a relative "curve."

Observational Learning

Observational learning, also called social learning theory, occurs when an observer's behaviour changes after viewing the behaviour of a model. An observer's behaviour can be affected by the positive or negative consequences—called vicarious reinforcement or vicarious punishment— of a model's behaviour.

There are several guiding principles behind observational learning, or social learning theory:

The observer will imitate the model's behaviour if the model possesses characteristics— things such as talent, intelligence, power, good looks, or popularity—that the observer finds attractive or desirable.

The observer will react to the way the model is treated and mimic the model's behaviour. When the model's behaviour is rewarded, the observer is more likely to reproduce the rewarded behaviour. When the model is punished, an example of vicarious punishment, the observer is less likely to reproduce the same behaviour.

A distinction exists between an observer's "acquiring" a behaviour and "performing" a behaviour. Through observation, the observer can acquire the behaviour without performing it. The observer may then later, in situations where there is an incentive to do so, display the behaviour.

Learning by observation involves four separate processes:

— *Attention:* Observers cannot learn unless they pay attention to what's happening around them. This process is influenced by characteristics of the model, such as how much one likes or identifies with the model, and by characteristics of the observer, such as the observer's expectations or level of emotional arousal.

— *Retention:* Observers must not only recognise the observed behaviour but also remember it at some later time. This process depends on the observer's ability to code or structure the information in an easily remembered form or to mentally or physically rehearse the model's actions.

— *Production:* Observers must be physically and/ intellectually capable of producing the act. In many cases the observer possesses the necessary responses. But sometimes, reproducing the model's actions may involve skills the observer has not yet acquired. It is one thing to carefully watch a circus juggler, but it is quite another to go home and repeat those acts.

— *Motivation:* In general, observers will perform the act only if they have some motivation or reason to do so. The presence of reinforcement or punishment, either to the model or directly to the observer, becomes most important in this process.

Attention and retention account for acquisition or learning of a model's behaviour; production and motivation control the performance.

Human development reflects the complex interaction of the person, the person's behaviour, and the environment. The relationship between these elements is called *reciprocal determinism*. A person's cognitive abilities, physical characteristics, personality, beliefs, attitudes, and so on influence both his or her behaviour and environment. These influences are reciprocal, however. A person's behaviour can affect his feelings about himself and his attitudes and beliefs about others. Likewise, much of what a person knows comes from environmental resources such as television, parents, and books. Environment also affects behaviour: what a person observes can powerfully influence what he does. But a person's behaviour also contributes to his environment.

Observational Learning Impacts Learning:

- *Curriculum:* Students must get a chance to observe and model the behaviour that leads to a positive reinforcement.
- *Instruction:* Educators must encourage collaborative learning, since much of learning happens within important social and environmental contexts.
- *Assessment:* A learned behaviour often cannot be performed unless there is the right environment for it. Educators must provide the incentive and the supportive environment for the behaviour to happen. Otherwise, assessment may not be accurate.

Vygotsky and Social Cognition

The social cognition learning model asserts that culture is the prime determinant of individual development. Humans are the only species to have created culture, and every human child develops in the context of a culture. Therefore, a child's learning development is affected in ways large and small by the culture—including the culture of family environment—in which he or she is enmeshed.

— Culture makes two sorts of contributions to a child's intellectual development. *First,* through culture children acquire much of the content of their thinking, that is, their knowledge. *Second,* the surrounding culture provides a child with the processes or means of their thinking, what Vygotskians call the tools of intellectual adaptation. In short, according to the social cognition learning model, culture teaches children both what to think and how to think.

— Cognitive development results from a dialectical process whereby a child learns through problem-solving experiences shared with someone else, usually a parent or teacher but sometimes a sibling or peer.

— Initially, the person interacting with child assumes most of the responsibility for guiding the problem solving, but gradually this responsibility transfers to the child.

— Language is a primary form of interaction through which adults transmit to the child the rich body of knowledge that exists in the culture.

— As learning progresses, the child's own language comes to serve as her primary tool of intellectual adaptation. Eventually, children can use internal language to direct their own behaviour.

— Internalisation refers to the process of learning—and thereby internalising—a rich body of knowledge and tools of thought that first exist outside the child. This happens primarily through language.

— A difference exists between what child can do on her own and what the child can do with help. Vygotskians call this difference the zone of proximal development.

— Since much of what a child learns comes form the culture around her and much of the child's problem solving is mediated through an adult's help, it is wrong to focus on a child in isolation. Such focus does not reveal the processes by which children acquire new skills.

— Interactions with surrounding culture and social agents, such as parents and more competent peers, contribute significantly to a child's intellectual development.

Vygotsky Impacts Learning

— *Curriculum:* Since children learn much through interaction, curricula should be designed to emphasize interaction between learners and learning tasks.

— *Instruction:* With appropriate adult help, children can often perform tasks that they are incapable of completing on their own. With this in mind, scaffolding—where the adult continually adjusts the level of his or her help in response to the child's level of performance—is an effective form of teaching. Scaffolding not only produces immediate results, but also instills the skills necessary for independent problem solving in the future.

— *Assessment*: Assessment methods must take into account the zone of proximal development. What children can do on their own is their level of actual development and what they can do with help is their level of potential development. Two children might have the same level of actual development, but given the appropriate help from an adult, one might be able to solve many more problems than the other. Assessment methods must target both the level of actual development and the level of potential development.

Organisational Theory

Total Quality Schools

Total Quality schools apply the principles and practices of Total Quality Management to their administrative and instructional functions.

When introduced in schools, the Total Quality process usually involves a combination of the following elements:

— *Understanding Systems and Processes*: Education administrators make efforts to understand their school as a system containing many subsystems and processes. To do so, they often will "map" their systems and "flowchart" their processes. Schools will then strive to improve by redesigning their systems.

— *Using Data for Decision-Making*: Employees learn to use data in decision-making. This frequently involves employing statistical methods to understand why processes vary.

— *Using Problem-Solving Teams and Teamwork*: Classroom teams use common problem-solving processes and tools to tackle challenges and improve procedures. Students are often taught to use both methods and tools to improve classroom operations.

— *Identifying and Understanding Customer Needs*: Schools identify the constituencies they need to satisfy, and attempt to understand their expectations and needs.

Schools will develop measurement systems that compare their performance to their constituents' expectations.

— *Quality Planning*: Some schools use quality planning processes as a supplement to their strategic planning processes for identifying and achieving organization-wide goals. This will often involve developing organization-wide quality indicators, or "scoreboards".

Charter Schools

In concept, a charter school is a self-governing, publicly funded school that the community holds accountable for the results it produces—such as student learning—rather than for its compliance with school board or government rules and regulations.

A charter school operates without the typical restraints of an ordinary public school, for example, collective-bargaining agreements. Its enrollment is made up of students who want to attend that specific school—in effect, a charter school is a school of choice. In addition to its unique legal and governance structure, a charter school takes on elements of site-based management: People at the school site have the power to make critical decisions about issues such as budget and personnel.

By January 1994, eight states had passed laws permitting the creation of charter schools. However, there are significant differences among these laws:

— Some states limit chartering to existing public schools that want to convert to charter status, while others allow the creation of new schools.

— Some states give responsibility for negotiating and approving charters to local school boards, while others bypass the local boards and allow entities such as community colleges, universities, and the state board of education to authorize charter schools.

— Some states cap the number of charter schools that can be created, and some do not. Plus, some states give charter schools blanket waivers from existing state rules and regulations, while other states require rule-by-rule negotiations.

Accelerated Schools

In 1986, Stanford University introduced the concept of accelerated schools, an approach designed to create success for **all** students by closing the achievement gap between at-risk and mainstream children. The idea is to radically change individual schools by redesigning and integrating curricular, instructional, and organizational practices so that they provide enrichment—not just remediation—for at-risk students.

The accelerated schools program assumes that at-risk students have "learning gaps" in areas valued by schools and mainstream economic and social institutions. The program also assumes that remedial approaches fail to close these gaps because they don't build on the students' strengths and they don't tap into the resources of teachers, parents, and the community.

When the accelerated schools program is introduced into a school, the process involves several guiding principles and values:

— *Unity of Purpose*: Parents, teachers, students, and administrators must agree on a common set of goals for the school. These goals become the focal point of everyone's efforts, serving as a framework for all curricular, instructional, and organizational initiatives.

— *Empowerment/Responsibility*: Members of the school

community can make important educational decisions, take responsibility for implementing them, and take responsibility for the outcomes. This breaks the stalemate among administrators, teachers, parents, and students: It stops them from blaming each other and factors beyond their control for the students' poor educational outcomes.

— *Building on Strengths*: This program identifies and uses all the available learning resources in the school community, instead of exaggerating weaknesses and ignoring strengths. For example, parents can positively influence their children's education at home and help teachers understand their children better. School administrators could make a concerted effort to creatively work with parents, staff, and students, rather than merely complying with them. Plus, teachers bring valuable insights, intuition, teaching, and organizational skills to the table. Furthermore, the strengths of at-risk students differ from those associated with predominantly white, middle-class culture, and often are overlooked. And finally, communities are ripe with assets, including youth organizations, senior citizens, businesses, religious groups.

Getting Started as an Accelerated School

There are four initial steps for developing an accelerated school. They are:

— Take stock of where you are, and establish baseline data.

— Create a shared vision as a focus for change.

— Compare your vision to baseline information, then identify gaps and needed changes.

— Identify 3-4 initial priorities, and establish small groups to work on these.

Comer Schools

This is an approach to restructuring the governance and practices of individual schools, initiated by psychologist James Comer in the mid-1970s. This approach hinges on Comer's theory of how children develop and learn, and the reasons that disadvantaged, minority children do not learn in schools.

Comer believes that children follow a developmental continuum. They are born, totally dependent, into a family that is part of a social network with beliefs, attitudes, activities, and lifestyles. Parents become mediators who tell children what is important. Children gradually learn to manage their feelings and impulses, in essence, to control themselves. Development occurs in speech and language, cognition, intellectual and academic understanding, and moral, psychological, and social dimensions. To learn, children must imitate and identify with authority figures, in other words, internalize attitudes and values by relating emotionally to others.

When children come to school prepared to learn in that school's style, due to how they have fared in the developmental continuum, they are perceived as "good." When they do not, they are often perceived as "bad." For this reason, Corner attests individual schools must support further developmental growth.

When the Comer process is introduced into a school, it usually involves the following elements:

— *Changed School Governance*: Parents, community members, teachers, administrators, and school staff collaborate in making key educational decisions.

— *Creation of a Social Skills Curriculum*: Schools need developmental programs for young children who do not learn certain types of skills at home. Typically, a social skills curriculum covers politics and government, business and economics, health and nutrition, and spiritual and leisure activities.

— *Adoption of a Developmental Perspective Toward Children and Their Learning*: This perspective incorporates three beliefs:

  — All children are capable of learning.

  — Learning is best achieved through the collaborative participation of all involved adults.

  — Students enter school at different points along a developmental continuum.

2

Instructional Theories

Mastery learning proposes that all children can learn when provided with the appropriate learning conditions in the classroom.

The application of mastery learning is based on Benjamin Bloom's Learning for Mastery model, with refinements made by Block. Mastery learning is predominantly a group-based, teacher-paced instructional approach, in which students learn by cooperating with their classmates. However, some mastery learning strategies require students to work independently, rather than with classmates.

Mastery Learning Affects Education

- *Curriculum*: Mastery learning does not focus on content, but on the process of mastering it. This type of learning works best with the traditional content-focused curriculum, one based on well-defined learning objectives organised into smaller, sequentially organised units.
- *Instruction*: This strategy captures many of the elements of successful tutoring and the independent functionality seen in high-end students. In a mastery learning environment, the teacher directs a variety of

group-based instructional techniques. The teacher also provides frequent and specific feedback by using diagnostic, formative tests, as well as regularly correcting mistakes students make along their learning path.

— *Assessment*: Teachers evaluate students with criterion-referenced tests rather then norm-referenced tests. Mastery learning ensures numerous feedback loops, based on small units of well-defined, appropriately sequenced outcomes.

Cooperative Learning

Cooperative learning consists of instructional techniques that require positive interdependence between learners in order for learning to occur.

Basic Elements

Competitive and cooperative interaction are a healthy part of a child's repertoire of behavior. By second grade, however, urban children have effectively extinguished their cooperative behavior and persist in competition, even when it's counterproductive. By developing deliberately cooperative techniques, educators aim to correct the unconscious societal and educational bias that favors competition.

Research has also found an interesting racial implication in cooperative learning: Minority children are more likely to retain these cooperative strategies. In fact, when educators introduce cooperative learning into the classroom, minority learners show a disproportionate improvement in achievement.

Patterns for student interaction are called structures. Together, teachers and students develop a repertoire of these structures. So when the teacher announces that the class will use a particular exercise to explore today's lesson topic, students know what type of interaction to expect. For example, when the teacher says the class will use the "Think-Pair-Share" exercise to study African wildlife, students know they will work independently to write down their thoughts on elephants or lions, then find a partner, share their ideas with their partner, and probe each other for complete understanding.

It is up to the instructor to integrate the interactive exercises with the specific lesson content. The teacher must give careful thought to who should collaborate with whom and why, how to manage the classroom while unleashing cooperative activity, and how to balance the attention to both content and cooperative skill building.

Accelerated Learning

Accelerated learning is a comprehensive approach to school change, developed in 1986 at Stanford University. Accelerated learning aims to create school success for **all** students by closing the achievement gap between at-risk and mainstream children. The idea is to radically change individual schools by redesigning and integrating curricular, instructional, and organisational practices so that they provide enrichment—not just remediation—for at-risk students.

The accelerated learning theory assumes that at-risk students have "learning gaps" in areas valued by schools and mainstream economic and social institutions. The program also assumes that remedial approaches fail to close these gaps because they don't build on the students' strengths and they don't tap into the resources of teachers, parents, and the community.

When an accelerated learning program is introduced into a school, the process involves several guiding principles and values:

— *Unity of Purpose*: Parents, teachers, students, and administrators must agree on a common set of goals for the school. These goals become the focal point of everyone's efforts, serving as a framework for all curricular, instructional, and organisational initiatives.

— *Empowerment/Responsibility*: Members of the school community can make important educational decisions, take responsibility for implementing them, and take responsibility for the outcomes. This breaks the stalemate among administrators, teachers, parents, and students: It stops them from blaming each other and factors beyond their control for the students' poor educational outcomes.

— *Building on Strengths*: This program identifies and uses all the available learning resources in the school community, instead of exaggerating weaknesses and ignoring strengths. For example, parents can positively influence their children's education at home and help teachers understand their children better. School administrators could make a concerted effort to creatively work with parents, staff, and students, rather than merely complying with them. Plus, teachers bring valuable insights, intuition, teaching, and organisational skills to the table. Furthermore, the strengths of at-risk students differ from those associated with predominantly white, middle-class culture, and often are overlooked. And finally, communities are ripe with assets, including youth organisations, senior citizens, businesses, religious groups.

Getting Started as an Accelerated School There are four initial steps for developing an accelerated school. They are:

— Take stock of where you are, and establish baseline data.
— Create a shared vision as a focus for change.
— Compare your vision to baseline information, then identify gaps and needed changes.
— Identify 3-4 initial priorities, and establish small groups to work on these.

Thematic Instruction

Thematic instruction is the organisation of a curriculum around macro "themes." Thematic instruction integrates basic disciplines like reading, math, and science with the exploration of a broad subject, such as communities, rain forests, river basins, the use of energy, and so on.

Thematic instruction is based on the idea that people acquire knowledge best when learning in the context of a coherent "whole," and when they can connect what they're learning to the real world. Thematic instruction seeks to put the teaching of cognitive skills such as reading, mathematics, science, and writing in the context of a real-world subject that is both specific enough to be practical, and broad enough to allow creative exploration.

Thematic instruction usually occurs within an entire grade level of students. Teachers of all the different subjects taught in that particular grade work together as a team to design curriculum, instruction methods, and assessment around a preselected theme. Typical steps include:

— *Choosing a theme*: Themes often involve a large, integrated system (such as a city, an ecosystem, and so on) or a broad concept (such as democracy, weather, and so on). Instructors often strive to connect the theme to the students' everyday life. In some cases, students participate in choosing the theme or themes.

- *Designing the integrated curriculum*: The teachers involved must organise the learning objectives of their core curriculum (both process skills and content knowledge) around the theme. In the study of a river basin, for instance, math might involve calculating water flow and volume; social studies could look at the nature of river communities; science might study phenomena like weather and floods; and literature could study books and novels that focus on rivers, such as the works of Mark Twain. The initial design requires considerable work on the part of teachers. Again, sometimes students help design the curriculum.
- *Designing the instruction*: This usually involves making changes to the class schedule, combining hours normally devoted to specific topics, organising field trips, teaching in teams, bringing in outside experts, and so on.
- *Encouraging presentation and celebration*: Because thematic instruction is often project-oriented, it frequently involves students giving collective presentations to the rest of the school or the community. Plus, students commonly create extensive visual displays.

Thematic instruction can be a powerful tool for reintegrating the curriculum and eliminating the isolated, reductionist nature of teaching around disciplines rather than experience. It requires a lot of hard, initial design work, plus a substantial restructuring of teacher relationships and class schedules.

Whole Brain Teaching

Whole-brain teaching is an instructional approach

derived from neurolinguistic descriptions of the functions of the brain's left and right hemispheres.

Neurolinguistic findings about the brain's language functions show that in the integrated brain, the functions of one hemisphere are immediately available to the other, producing a more balanced use of language. Whole-brain teaching emphasizes active learning, in which the learner makes connections that tap both hemispheres.

Another aspect of whole-brain teaching is managing the emotional climate, to reduce the "downshifting"—or primal thinking—that occurs during distress. To relax learners, instructors may offer clear, realistic predictions of barriers (such as, "Advancement may be sporadic") and progress (such as, "Sooner or later, this will become easier"). Plus, instructors may try enhancing the learning experience with music or soothing colors.

In whole-brain learning, imaging is seen as the basis for comprehension. For this reason, learners are encouraged to visualise, draw, and use drama as they develop new ideas, in order to retain them. A reading teacher, for instance, might present new vocabulary words by building a story or skit that uses them—but doesn't define them—in context. The teacher then might play music while reading the definitions, leaving time for listeners to draw images of the words. The teacher next might use guided meditation to build a relaxed state containing memories of success before the listeners hear the definitions again. And the learners might even act out the words' meanings or construct stories of their own.

Service Learning

Service learning combines service to the community with learning outside the classroom. Schools throughout the country are striving to implement service learning along the entire K-12 continuum.

Service learning has acquired several different meanings. For instance, some high schools have instituted a requisite that all students must perform a certain number of hours of community service. Other schools have implemented service learning as a part of their ongoing curriculum. This may include class, team, or individual exercises and assignments. For example, a project might revolve around cleaning up trash in a park, categorising the waste, and determining its impact on the environment.

And some schools even employ programs in which individual students serve the community organisations that relate to their career interests.

Service Learning Affects Education

— *Curriculum*—Depending on the definition of service learning, there can be a significant impact on curriculum. Schools use service learning to provide meaning and context to the information taught. However, students that merely volunteer for community service hours may have little impact on what happens in the classroom. Those students who do see connections—or a lack of them—between the concepts learned and their real-world applications may pressure schools for curriculum changes of context and relevancy.

— *Instruction*—Teachers may need to expand their own knowledge base to extend learning beyond the classroom. Teachers may also have to relinquish their perception as being the only source of information. The goals of instruction often change from amassing knowledge to using and applying knowledge in a real-world context.

— *Assessment*—Service learning often changes the

nature of assessment by focusing on the customer satisfaction of the organisation students are serving. Teacher's assessment can be either shared or replaced by assessors in the community who can provide more accurate feedback.

Cognitive Coaching

Cognitive coaching is based on the idea that metacognition—or being aware of one's own thinking processes—fosters independence in learning. By providing personal insights into the learner's own thinking processes, cognitive coaching builds flexible, confident problem-solving skills. Plus, it encourages self-efficacy and pride.

Coaching involves the modeling of self-appraisal and the self-management of cognition by an expert. It also involves learner performance and reflection, internalising, and generalising.

In modeling, the instructor explains thinking, reading, and calculating strategies by naming the strategy (such as "eliminating alternatives" or "finding the main idea"), then explaining why it should be learned. The instructor also provides explicit steps for using a particular strategy, deciding when it's appropriate, and evaluating it.

Dialogue, both on the part of instructor and student, is another prominent aspect of coaching. For example, in the "scaffolded instruction" technique, teachers and students take turns leading dialogues about texts, asking each other to predict, question, clarify, summarise, and self-appraise.

Scott Paris, in his 1990 article "Promoting Metacognition and Motivation of Exceptional Children" in *Remedial and Special Education,* lists the following fundamentals of building effective metacognitive skills:

- Common goals held by teachers and students
- Ongoing assessment of performance, in order to adjust difficulty levels
- Mutual regulation—in other words, teachers benefit from the students' misconceptions and observations of the strategies, while students learn from their instructor's previous experience using the strategies

Adult learning principles greatly support cognitive coaching and predict its success. For example, adult coaching is often used as an alternative to clinical supervision in developing the teaching and management skills of school administrators. However, cognitive coaching is also being developed in K-12 instructional programs for special needs and whole language students. Apparently, the same principles apply for both adults and children...imagine that!

School to Work Transition

School-to-work programs provide ways for students to transition successfully into the economy, either through paid employment with a business or self-employment. Numerous studies reveal that, upon high school graduation, many students who aren't college-bound are neither prepared for nor connected to employment opportunities.

In general, building a school-to-work transition program entails the following three approaches:

- *Integrate the long-separated "tracks" of academic and vocational education.* From middle school on, schools should orient youth to work, help them explore different types of jobs, provide guidance about career paths, and assist them in finding work relevant to their needs and interests. Vocational education is considered too narrow and specific, outdated by modern technology, and ineffective in building language and math skills. Academic education is criticised for being too conventional, driven predominantly by standardised tests, and ineffective at motivating most students.

— *Link schooling with the demands and realities of the workplace.* Through employment-related experiences and on-the-job learning, students can receive significant exposure to the workforce and can prepare for their future work environment.

— *Develop programs to closely coordinate secondary and post-secondary education with employers.* Apprenticeships and school-business partnerships are just two of the many ways educators and businesspeople can produce a shared view of youth learning and development.

These changes have extensive learning implications, particularly for high schools, including:

— *Curriculum*—Develop new models that integrate vocational and academic education, from revamping the guidance counseling system to creating a coherent sequence of courses related to broad occupational clusters.

— *Instruction*—Focus on experiential, project-based learning. Also, reduce the "tracking," or segregation, of students into either academic or vocational studies.

— *Assessment*—Use portfolios to gauge a student's employability.

Instructional Technology

Instructional technology is just what it sounds like: using computers, CD-ROMs, interactive media, modems, satellites, teleconferencing, and other technological means to support learning.

Some educators believe the use of interactive, computer-based technology is crucial to improving classroom learning. These educators contend that advanced technology will fundamentally change the learning process and structure. Other educators believe technology is merely a tool that has minimal impact on the quality of learning.

Instructional Technology Affects Learning

- *Curriculum*: Advanced technology has the potential to significantly expand the breadth and depth of the curriculum. With the Internet, for example, students can access information far beyond the scope of their traditional textbooks. Curricula can be individualised and adapted to students' specific learning styles. Instructional technology has the power to enhance overall knowledge accumulation, instead of just focusing on content mastery.
- *Instruction*: Advanced technology could significantly affect the role of teachers, as well as the structure of schools and classrooms. The use of instructional technology changes the teacher's role from expert to facilitator or coach. Plus, instruction is no longer limited to the school building or classroom. For example, students can take courses from a global satellite feed or on the Internet. Learning can take place at home, at work, or anywhere else that has the capacity for a television, phone, or computer.
- *Assessment*: Instructional technology will focus more and more on building feedback loops directly into the learning process. Students can obtain frequent and accurate feedback, make corrections to their work, and structure learning experiences around

their individual needs. Assessment can be monitored by offsite instructors, plus it can be ongoing and cumulative.

Youth Apprenticeship

Youth apprenticeship is a learning system that prepares students for work by giving them a combination of classroom instruction and paid on-the-job training. In this education model, students obtain a set of well-defined occupational abilities by learning concepts in the classroom and applications in a work setting.

Youth apprenticeship systems in the U.S. have been influenced by successful apprenticeship models in Germany, Denmark, Switzerland, and Austria. About 66% of the youth in these European countries use an apprenticeship system to prepare for the workforce.

Apprenticeships range in occupation from baking to banking. Apprenticeship systems are run by a partnership of government, educators, and employers. Employer committees play a significant role in designing, monitoring, and evaluating apprenticeship programs. Programs begin accepting youth at age 15 or 16 (once they have finished their requisite education), and run for three to four years.

U.S. policy makers have been trying to develop a youth apprenticeship system that is more flexible and fits into our nation's structure of education, governance, and business.

Youth Apprenticeship Affects Learning

— *Curriculum:* The curriculum for specific occupational skills generally has been perceived as rather narrow. This is because content in the classroom mainly focuses on the applications called for in the workplace. However, most European apprenticeship programs have broadened their curriculum to focus more heavily on technology, critical thinking, problem solving, teamwork, and project management.

— *Instruction:* In the past, the popular opinion has been that academic instruction in apprenticeship—and other occupational—programs is neglected or weak. However, today there is a strong movement to add rigorous academic standards to apprenticeship programs, and to integrate the academic activities with the occupational skill training. Instruction at the work site varies: Some sites offer very formal and prescribed programs, while others provide informal mentoring by a master in the trade or profession. Critics charge that large companies tend to replicate classroom or laboratory training without providing much hands-on learning, while small companies often exploit apprentices as cheap labor without offering much real instruction.

— *Assessment:* Assessment in the academic classrooms has traditionally relied on tests and grades. In the occupational laboratories, however, assessment includes a combination of traditional testing and project completion. At the workplace, assessment is generally authentic and includes feedback from supervisors, mentors, and co-workers. Since students are working while learning, there is continual feedback on the quality of their efforts.

Models of Instructional Designs

Models, like myths and metaphors, help us to make sense of our world. Whether derived from whim or from serious research, a model offers its user a means of comprehending an otherwise incomprehensible problem.

An instructional design model gives structure and meaning to an I.D. problem, enabling the would-be designer to negotiate her design task with a semblance of conscious understanding. Models help us to visualise the problem, to break it down into discrete, manageable units.

The value of a specific model is determined within the context of use. Like any other instrument, a model assumes a specific intention of its user. A model should be judged by how it mediates the designer's intention, how well it can share a work load, and how effectively it shifts focus away from itself toward the object of the design activity.

Instructional Design is the systematic development of instructional specifications using learning and instructional theory to ensure the quality of instruction. It is the entire process of analysis of learning needs and goals and the development of a delivery system to meet those needs. It includes development of instructional materials and activities; and tryout and evaluation of all instruction and learner activities.

Instructional Design is that branch of knowledge concerned with research and theory about instructional strategies and the process for developing and implementing those strategies.

Instructional design is the science of creating detailed specifications for the development, implementation, evaluation, and maintenance of situations that facilitate the learning of both large and small units of subject matter at all levels of complexity.

Instructional design can start at any point in the design process. Often a glimmer of an idea is developed to give the core of an instruction situation. By the time the entire process is done the designer looks back and she or he checks to see that all parts of the "science" have been taken into account. Then the entire process is written up as if it occurred in a systematic fashion.

Instructional System

An instructional system is an arrangement of resources and procedures to promote learning. Instructional design is the systematic process of developing instructional systems and instructional development is the process of implementing the system or plan.

Instructional Technology

Instructional technology is the systemic and systematic application of strategies and techniques derived from behavioral, cognitive, and constructivist theories to the solution of instructional problems. Instructional technology is the systematic application of theory and other organised knowledge to the task of instructional design and development.

Instructional Technology = Instructional Design + Instructional Development

History

As a formal discipline, Instructional Systems Design has been a long time in the making. The early contributions of thinkers such as Aristotle, Socrates and Plato regarding the cognitive basis of learning and memory was later expanded by the 13th century philosopher St. Thomas Aquinas who discussed the perception of teachings in terms of free will. Four hundred years later, John Locke advanced Aristotle's notion of human's initial state of mental blankness by proposing that almost all reason and knowledge must be gained from experience. Then, at the turn of the 20th century John Dewey presented several tenets of the philosophy of education which promoted the idea that learning occurs best when married with *doing,* rather than rote regurgitation of facts.

As the 1920's approached, a behaviorist approach to educational psychology became increasingly predominant. Thorndike's theory of connectionism represents the original stimulus-response (S-R) model of behavioral psychology, and was expanded on some twenty years later by Hull in his exposition of drive reduction – a motivational model of behavior which emphasizes learner's wants, attention, and activities. With the Industrial Revolution came an increased attention to productivity, and educational behaviorists during the 1920's such as Sidney Pressey applied mechanised technology to increase the efficiency of the learning process. Though their initial incarnation did not see much use after the Depression, many of the lessons learned research into these teaching machines regarding the delivery of standardised instruction contributed to the instructional media research & development movement of World War II.

The advent of the Second World War presented a tremendous instructional dilemma: the rapid training of hundreds of thousands of military personnel. Ralph Tyler's work a decade before WWII indicated that objectives were most useful to instructional developers if written in terms of desired learner behaviors. Armed with this knowledge and the experience of creating standardise methods of instructional delivery using teaching machines, military researchers developed a bevy of training films and other mediated materials for instructional purposes. In part, the United States' heavy investment in training and R&D was credited with the country's victory in the war. With the economic boom that followed, federal dollars followed researcher's desire to better flesh out the underpinnings of learning, cognition, and instruction.

The 1950's are characterised by a shift away from the uninformed application of instructional technology to the formulation of theoretical models of learning. The publication of B. F. Skinner's *The Science of Learning and the Art of Teaching* in 1954 canonised the basic behaviorist principles of S-R, feedback, and reinforcement. As the key element of his theory of operant conditioning, the reinforcement of desired learner responses was also incorporated into Skinner's implementations of programmed instruction. Considered by many the progenitor of contemporary instructional design, programmed instruction emphasizes the formulation of behavioral objectives, breaking instructional content into small units and rewarding correct responses early and often.

Another substantial instructional theorist of the 1950's was Benjamin Bloom. His 1956 taxonomy of intellectual behaviors provided instructors a means by which to decide how to impart instructional content to learners most effectively. Advocating a mastery approach to learning, Bloom endorsed instructional techniques that varied both instruction and time according to learner requirements. While this approach provided instructional developers a means by which to match subject matter and instructional methods, Bloom's taxonomy was not in and of itself capable of satisfying the desire of large organizations to relate resources and processes to the performances of individuals.

To achieve this researchers in the military's Air Research and Development Command borrowed from Ludwig von Bertalanffy's General Systems Theory of biological interactions to integrate the operations of a wide range of departments, such as training, intelligence, and staffing. Combined with the Bloom's Taxonomy, the systems approach to instructional and organisational development allowed planners and policy-makers to match the content and delivery of instruction in a fashion which considered both super- and sub-systems (the organisation as a whole, as well as groups and individuals within the organisation). These advances of Skinner, Bloom and von Bertalanffy were usually employed to develop instruction in what was only *assumed* to be an effective an efficient manner. The formalisation of a standardised design process still had yet to be devised.

Again it was a crisis that spurred the next evolution of instructional technology – a shift away from an emphasis in the development of instructional programs to one which focused on the design of entire curriculum. Again the crisis was a war, but this time the war was a political one. In 1957 the Soviet Union launched the Sputnik satellite and began the "space race". America was taken by surprise and the government was forced to reevaluate the education system and its shortcomings. Science and math programs were the first to be targeted, and the government employed experts in these fields to bring the content up to date.

In 1962 Robert Glaser synthesised the work of previous researchers and introduced the concept of "instructional design", submitting a model which links learner analysis to the design and development of instruction. Interestingly, Glaser's contribution to the current field of instructional systems is not so much in the advancement of his model, but in work concerning Individually Prescribed Instruction (IPI), an approach whereby the results of a learner's placement test are used to plan learner-specific instruction.

At the same time Glaser was developing his theories of instructional design and IPI, Robert Mager published his treatise on the construction of performance objectives. Mager suggested that an objective should describe in measurable terms who an objective targets, the behavior they will have exhibited, the conditions or limitations under which they must carry out this behavior, and the criteria against which their behavior will be gauged.

As early as 1962 when he published "Military Training and Principles of Learning" Robert Gagné demonstrated a concern for the different levels of learning. His differentiation of psychomotor skills, verbal information, intellectual skills, cognitive strategies, and attitudes provides a companion to Bloom's six cognitive domains of learning. Later, Gagné extended his thinking to include nine instructional events that detail the conditions necessary for learning to occur. These events have long since been used for the basis for the design of instruction and the selection of appropriate media.

The mediation of instruction entered the computer age in the 1960's when Patrick Suppes conducted his initial investigations into computer-assisted instruction (CAI) at Stanford University. Developed through a systematic analysis of curriculum, Suppes' CAI provided learner feedback, branching, and response tracking – aspects were later incorporated into the PLATO system in the 1970's and continue guide the development of today's instructional software.

By the late 1960's America was again in crisis. Not only was the country involved in another war, but the nation's schools were unable to elicit the achievement from learners it anticipated. Grant Venn argued that since only 19% of first graders complete a bachelor or arts degree, that the current educational system is only serving the advantaged minority of schoolchildren. To counter this trend Robert Morgan proposed to conduct an experiment with an "organic curriculum" which would to incorporate into the educational system the best instructional practices identified through research. Accepted in 1967 the proposal by the US Office of Education, the project was dubbed "Educational Systems for the 1970's", or ES'70.

Morgan engaged an array of experts in the field of learning, cognition, and instructional design to contribute to the project and carried out multiple experiments in a variety of settings. Of these was Leslie Briggs, who had demonstrated that an instructionally designed course could yield up to 2:1 increase over conventionally designed courses in terms of achievement, reduction in variance, and reduction of time-to-completion – this effect was four times that of the control group which received no training.

In 1970, Morgan partnered with the Florida Research and Development Advisory Board to conduct a nation-wide educational reform project in South Korea. Faced with the task of increasing the achievement of learners while at the same time *reducing* the cost of schooling from $41.27 per student per year Morgan applied some of the same techniques as had been piloted in the ES'70 project and achieved striking results: an increase in student achievement, a more efficient organisation of instructors and course content, an increased teacher to student ratio, a reduction in salary cost, and a reduction in yearly per student cost by $9.80.

Around this time Roger Kaufman developed a problem-solving framework for educational strategic planning which provided practitioners a means by which to demonstrate value-added not only for the learner, but the school system and society as a whole. This framework provided the basis for the Organisational Elements Model (OEM), a needs assessment model which specifies results to be achieved at societal, organisational, and individual performance levels.

By rigorously defining needs as gaps in results Kaufman emphasized that performance improvement interventions can not demonstrate return-on-investment unless those interventions were derived from the requirements of these three primary clients and beneficiaries of organisational action. This approach to needs assessment and strategic planning has since been used across the world as the foundation for planning, evaluation, and continuous improvement in military, business, and educational settings.

A variety of models for instructional system design proliferated the late 1970's and early 80's: Gagné and Briggs, Branson, Dick and Carey, and Atkins, to name a few. One possible reason for this phenomenon deals with the establishment of formal education and training departments within both public and private organisations. Faced with the computerised technologies of the times, these organisations require a means by which to quickly develop appropriate methods by which to educate internal employees in the new business practices ushered into existence by the Information Age.

Another explanation is that businesses, especially consulting organisations, are becoming increasingly required to demonstrate value-added not only to their organisation, but to the clients they serve. The evaluation and continuous improvement components of contemporary models of ISD make far strides from the early develop-and-implement models of the middle of the century in this aspect.

In the 1990's a dual focus on technology and performance improvement has developed. For example, in his 1988 essay "Why the Schools Can't Improve: The Upper Limit Hypothesis" Robert Branson offers an argument for systemic school reform, suggesting that schools are operating at near peak efficiency and must be redesigned from the top down using technological interventions. Later in that year Branson was contracted by the Florida Department of Education (DOE) to analyse it's various programs and plan a system-wide technology-based educational reform initiative for Florida called Schoolyear 2000. Over the next several years Branson's team developed and piloted multiple computerised instructional technologies, as well as models of the interaction between the internal operations of the school system and the experiences and knowledge of students, parents, and teachers.

Developments in performance improvement outside ISD during the 1990's such as Quality Management (QM), Organisational Engineering, and Change Management have required that instructional designers look outside their profession to demonstrate the utility of their practice. Introduced earlier by Deming, QM has swept public and private organisations alike in the 90's. Whereas initially thought of in terms of "quality control" or "zero defects", quality practices have evolved into tools for organisational continuous improvement.

Similarly, instructional designers in the 90's often work alongside authorities in the field of organisational engineering. Characterised by a concern for an organisation's culture and interaction between groups, organisational engineering seeks to improve organisations through the identification of relationships between an organisation's vision, mission, goals, methods and personnel. Similarly, change management has become a business in and of itself, with leaders such as Darly Conner and Joel Barker pioneering methods for and models of organisational change.

The advent of new media, such as the Internet and hypermedia, has brought about not only technological innovations, but also coupled these with new ways of approaching learning and instruction. As opposed to the behavioralist perspective that emphasizes learning objectives, the constructivist approach holds that learners construct their understanding of reality from interpretations of their experiences. Theorists such as Thomas Duffy and Seymour Papert suggest that constructivism provides a model whereby socio-cultural and cognitive issues regarding the design of learning environments can be supported by computer tools. This philosophy has been applied to such computerised technologies as online help systems and programming language LOGO.

In the future, instructional designers are likely to choose one of two paths: specialist or generalist. In the prior path, designers will focus on one aspect of learning or instruction and act as consultants or subject matter experts, whether internal or external to the organisation. The other approach is one more aligned with managerial activities. Since the field is becoming too broad for most designers to work with authority in all matters, this option allows practitioners to oversee the development of instructional projects, rather than narrow their efforts exclusively on assessment, analysis, design, development, implementation, evaluation or continuous improvement.

Instructional-design Theory

Instructional-design theories, of all theory bases, are those most often used by instructional designers. According to Reigeluth in the "green book," *Instructional-Design Theories and Models, Volume II*, an instructional-design theory is a theory that offers explicit guidance on how to better help people learn and develop. The concepts of learn and develop may include cognitive, emotional, social, physical, and spiritual.

Gagné and Dick describe instructional-design theories as: an attempt to relate specified events of instruction to learning processes and learning outcomes

— based on the knowledgebase of learning research and theory

— prescriptive in the sense that they attempt to identify conditions of instruction which will optimize learning, retention, and learning transfer

— expected to provide, at minimum, rational description of causal relationships between procedures used to teach and their behavioral outcomes, preferably enhanced human performance

Reigeluth describes the characteristics of an instructional-design theory as:

— An orientation towards design, focusing on the means to attain goals for learning and development. It is not description oriented, which emphasizes the results of given events, like the information-processing theory. Design oriented (or goal oriented) theories are practical and useful to educators, showing them how to achieve their goals. They are *prescriptive.*

— Identification of methods of instruction, which are ways to support and facilitate instruction, and the situations in which those methods should and should not be used. These two components are necessary for all instructional-design theory and indicate that methods are situational, not universal in application.

— The methods of instruction can be broken into more detailed component methods, which provide more guidance to educators. These parts' can be made up of smaller methods. The additional implication is methods have different 'kinds' of characteristics. Outcomes are dependent on the situation. 'Criteria' can be provided that the method should meet. The level of guidance can vary.

- The methods are probabilistic rather than deterministic, which means they increase the chances of attaining the goals rather than ensuring attainment of the goals. The goal of an instructional-design theory is to attain the highest possible probability of the desired results occurring.
- An instructional-design theory's goal (or design) has a value or philosophy that underlies it. Values play a key role in deciding what goals to pursue via the selection of methods offered to attain those goals.

For many graduate students in instructional design, the concept of an instructional design *model* is confusing. No doubt the imprecise use of terminology within the ISD field has lead to a large gray area of understanding. Instructional design models may be defined as the visualised representations of an instructional design process, showing the main elements or phases, and their relationships.

More commonly known by their names, Dick & Carey Model, ADDIE Model, Kemp Model, ICARE Model, and ASSURE Model, these models share three major activities: analysis, strategy development, and evaluation. I find it more useful to call these "systems" level models, instructional *systems design* models. (Just to add more confusion in the attempt to clarify!) Instructional design models, in my opinon, serve the needs of designers at the unit, course, or curriculum level.

Every model has some attributes not universally seen in all the others, such as inclusion of context analysis as a function of the design process, sequencing of test development, and the formative evaluation. Because of the limitations of two-dimensional graphic representations and to simplify a discussion of the activities of instructional design, the models have an unintended, yet starkly apparent attribute, sequentiality.

Designers from every experience level may sometimes follow this sequence; however, more commonly circumstances may cause the designer to modify the sequence of design activities. Many times the steps within a certain phase may occur concurrently. Considering the nature of the mental activity designers engage when implementing an instructional design model, the most accurate model would resemble an interwoven, nonlinear relationship of activity, like a knotted tapestry.

Educational Technology's Effect on Models of Instruction

In 1983, A Nation at Risk was published. It called attention to the serious problems of schooling in America. The major problem was that schools had not kept pace with society's expectations and needs for the rapidly changing world of the twenty first century.

Inorder to succeed in the twenty first century schools must graduate students who are prepared to be lifelong learners. This challenge necessitates a pedagogical shift from transmitting a body of expected knowledge that is largely memorised to one that is largely process oriented. For example, instead of having students memorise the names of the battles of the Civil War, a teacher might have teams of students each focus on one battle and prepare a presentation on it using first-hand letters, testimonies, and photos.

The concept of multiple intelligence comes into play here as well. Our traditional concept of intelligence include an overemphasis on verbally-loaded skills. Expanded views of intelligence are especially important because people's beliefs about the nature of intelligence can affect their assessment of their own capabilities and their actual performance. Howard Gardner lists the following seven areas of intelligence: linguistic, logical/

mathematical, musical, artistic, spatial, bodily/kinesthetic, interpersonal and intrapersonal. Giving students a chance to share a wide variety of kinds of intelligence adds to their confidence and belief in themselves as intelligent and competent learners, that no matter what the task they will be able to learn to do it.

Prior to 1970 Behavioral Psychology formed the basis of how many teachers behaved in the classroom. Coupled with the traditional body of knowledge that made up a 'good' education this approach made sense. Now a basis in Cognitive Psychology seems to be a better method for preparing students to become lifelong learners. Advances in educational technology have contributed and supported this swing toward the Cognitive approach.

Behavioral Approach

B.F. Skinner is considered the "grandfather of behaviorism". He generated much of the experimental data that is the basis of behavioral learning theory. He and other behavioral theorists were concerned mainly with observable indications of learning and what those observations could imply for teaching. They concentrated on observable 'cause and effect' relationships. Skinner and others viewed the teacher's job as modifying the behavior of students by setting up situations to reinforce students when they exhibit desired responses.

Behaviorists viewed learning as a sequence of stimulus and response actions in the learner. They reasoned that teachers could link together responses involving lower-level skills and create a learning "chain" to teach higher-level skills. The teacher would determine all of the skills needed to lead up to the desired behavior and make sure students learned them all in a step-by-step manner.

Cognitive Approach

Many educational psychologists found the behavioral approach unsatisfying. In the areas of problem solving and learning strategies they became more concerned with what was unobservable—what was going on inside the brain. These theories are based on the work of educational philosopher John Dewey, and educational psychologists Lev Vygotsky, Jean Piaget, Jerome Bruner among others. They propose that children actively construct knowledge and this construction of knowledge happens in a social context.

Vygotsky proposed that all learning takes place in the 'zone of proximal development'. This 'zone' is the difference between what a child can do alone and what he/she can do with assistance. By building on the child's experiences and providing moderately challenging tasks teachers can provide the 'intellectual scaffolding' to help children learn and progress through the different stages of development.

The methods of constructivism emphasize students' ability to solve real-life, practical problems. Students typically work in cooperative groups rather than individually; they tend to focus on projects that require solutions to problems rather than on instructional sequences that require learning of certain content skills. The job of the teacher in constructivist models is to arrange for required resources and act as a guide to students while they set their own goals and 'teach themselves'.

Models of Instruction

Educational technology is supporting specific techniques of teaching and learning. Because of this support, educators are able to accomplish behavioral and cognitive goals in ways they never could before.

Direct Instruction/Explicit Teaching

Direct Instruction, also known as Explicit Teaching "is a systematic method for presenting material in small steps, pausing to check for student understanding and eliciting active and successful participation from all students." This model of instruction is well grounded in Behaviorist Theory.

It has also been classified as a 'transmission' model (as opposed to an 'information-processing' model). Rosenshine details six teaching functions as an important sequence in the method of Explicit teaching.

They are: daily review, presenting new material, guided practice, corrections and feedback, independent practice and weekly and monthly reviews. This method has been shown to be particularly effective in the "teaching of mathematical procedures and computations, reading decoding, explicit reading procedures such as distinguishing fact from opinion, science facts and concepts, social science facts and concepts, map skills, foreign language vocabulary. They are less relevant for teaching in areas that are less well-structured, for example, teaching composition, reading comprehension, analysing literature or historical trends."

There are two major categories of educational technology that support this method of teaching. One of the first applications of computer software in the classroom was in the form of drill and practice programs. There are many that take the task of providing guided and independent practice to students.

Some are very straightforward, for example, *Jurassic Spelling* by DareWare and Motes Educational. This is a spelling practice program that provides verbal rewards every time a student spells a word correctly, after a student has accumulated a certain number of points he/

she is rewarded with a picture and information on a dinosaur.

Another example, *Animated Multiplication and Division* by Guthery and Meza. Here the scenario is similar when a student gets a certain number of math problems correct they are rewarded by being allowed to create a picture that the program will then animate. The program *Super Solvers: Outnumbered!* by The Learning Company is a very creative program for math concepts. Here word problems are given and students need to figure out how to solve the problem, they travel to different rooms solving problems in order to capture the villain. Feedback is given along the way.

Rewards come in the form of points scored at the end of the game. These practice programs can free the teacher to help other students. If used in a group setting they can provide the opportunity for students to collaborate, a more constructivist approach.

Another type of software that supports this model is the tutorial type of program. In a tutorial program instruction is usually expected to stand alone; the student should be able to learn the topic without any help or other materials from outside the courseware. Tutorials should address all instructional events i.e. all six teaching functions that Rosenshine defines. Tutorials can be categorised as linear or branching tutorials. A linear tutorial gives the same instructional sequence and feedback to all learners.

A branching tutorial directs learners along alternate paths depending on how they respond to questions and whether or not they show mastery of certain parts of the material. Emulating a good teacher is difficult for a person, let alone a computer, but there are some very good tutorials available. A good example is the tutorials that come with new computers or software, i.e. the

Introduction to Microsoft Works, or the *Tour of Windows 3.1*. Some other examples of tutorial software are *DaisyQuest* and *Daisy's Castle* by Great Wave software. They are "magical" auditory programs created especially for young children and for older children who may experience difficulty learning to read due to deficits in the ability to isolate and compare sounds in words.

Cooperative/Collaborative Learning

Cooperative (sometime known as Collaborative) Learning is a model of teaching with a set of common attributes and features. It is cognitive in nature. It also has several variations. The following are its essential features: students work in teams to master academic materials, teams are made up of high, average, and low achievers, and are racially and sexually mixed, reward systems are group-oriented rather than individually oriented. Some of the variations are:

Student Teams Achievement Divisions (STAD) where team members use work sheets or other study devices to master the academic materials and then help each other learn the material. Individually students take weekly quizzes and are given an "improvement score". This score is based on the degree to which the score exceeds a student's past average. Teams strive to get a good team improvement score.

Jigsaw where each student on the team would be responsible to become 'an expert' in one aspect of the academic task and are responsible for teaching that aspect to the others. Members from different teams who are to be experts on the same topic meet to help each other learn their aspect of the task. They then return to their group to share what they learned and plan their presentation to the class.

Group Investigation where students are involved in planning both the topics for study and the ways to proceed with their investigation. Students will choose a topic for study, proceed with an in-depth investigation of that topic and prepare and present a report to the whole class.

There are two types of technology that support Cooperative Learning. The first category includes those types of programs that will provide the environment for collaboration. Included here are the types of software that we usually think of as tools: word processors (*Word, WordPerfect*), spreadsheets(*Excel, Lotus 1-2-3*), data bases(*Access, FoxPro*), drawing programs(*Corel Draw, Paintbrush*), desk top publishing programs (*Microsoft Publisher, Print Shop*) script writing tools (*Hollywood High, 3D Movie Maker*) Multimedia Presentations(*Power Point, Hyperstudio, Poduim*).

Each of these tools provide the environment for students to produce a product that they can share with the class or publish in a newsletter to parents or publish on the World Wide Web to the world. No matter which program students use they must make important decisions together on what information to convey and how to convey it. Learning content material, learning to work together, and valuing each other for their multiple intelligence are all goals of cooperative learning that teachers can focus on in this environment.

There are many programs that will provide the resources that students need to complete the research that is needed for class presentations. There are several very good multimedia encyclopedias. There are many informative CD's on a wide variety of subject areas, Medio's *JFK Investigation*, DK Multimedia's *The Way Things Work*, Mindscapes's *How Your Body Works*, Research Publications' *American Journey* to name just a few. These programs can collect an enormous amount of information that is easily searched and copied into word processors for use as notes to share with fellow teammates.

The Internet is a resource of hundreds of thousands of documents on any subject imaginable. By using the search engines, Alta Vista or Yahoo, for example, a student can find much information on virtually any topic. Some instruction and class discussion on techniques for searching and evaluation of sources is needed to get the most of working in this environment. When we view our task of encouraging students to be lifelong learners, these become indispensable tools. The WWW is also a great resource for the pictures and sounds that go into making a great classroom presentation. The Lycos search engine has the capability to search the web for these resources.

Cognitive Apprenticeship

Cognitive Apprenticeship is a method of teaching aimed primarily at teaching the processes that experts use to handle complex tasks. The focus of this learning-through-guided-experience is on cognitive and metacognitive skills, rather than on the physical skills and processes of traditional apprenticeships. Applying apprenticeship methods to largely cognitive skills requires the externalisation of processes that are usually carried out internally. Observing the processes by which an expert listener or reader thinks and practices these skills can teach students to learn on their own more skillfully. This method includes:

— Modeling: involves an expert's carrying out a task so that student can observe and build a conceptual model of the processes that are required to accomplish the task. For example, a teacher might model the reading process by reading aloud in one voice, while verbalising her thought processes (summarise what she just read, what she thinks might happen next) in another voice.

— *Coaching:* consists of observing students while they carry out a task and offering hints, feedback, modeling, reminders, etc.

— *Articulation:* includes any method of getting students to articulate their knowledge, reasoning, or problem-solving processes.

— *Reflection:* enables students to compare their own problem-solving processes with those of an expert or another student.

— *Exploration:* involves pushing students into a mode of problem solving on their own. Forcing them to do exploration is critical, if they are to learn how to frame questions or problems that are interesting and that they can solve.

Support from technology in this area has blossomed from the Internet. Through special programs or Cybrid CDs students are able to connect to real experts in a discipline as mentors.

One such special program is the Electronic Emissary Project at the University of Texas at Austin. It is a match-maker that brings together teachers, students, and subject-matter authorities in a digital exchange of ideas. Some examples of the pairs that have been matched are these:

Fourth and fifth graders in Kansas City, Missouri, learned about writing and broadcasting news from Vance Elderkin, a lecturer in the Department of Communications at North Caroling State University

High school seniors in Windsor, Connecticut, discuss and research current events with the help of B. Welling

Hall, a political science professor at Earlham college in Columbus, Ohio.

The Cybrid CD combines all the bells and whistles users have come to expect from CD-ROM technology with a direct and ideally, seamless, connection to the internet. Although this new product is still fairly open, some of the cybrid CDs allow users to connect with experts to get help.

For example in MathSoft's *StudyWorks!* educators and secondary-level students can find a comprehensive set of services, including homework mentors, a forum for original papers and links to thousands of organisations and experts. *The Ultimate Medical Guide* (IV Publishing) adds immediacy and interaction to its CD by taking users to the Mayo Health O@sis site for a chance to talk directly to doctors, dietitians, and other Mayo Clinic staff .

Discovery Learning

Jerome Bruner was influential in defining Discovery Learning. It uses Cognitive psychology as a base. Discovery learning is "an approach to instruction through which students interact with their environment-by exploring and manipulating objects, wrestling with questions and controversies, or performing experiments" The idea is that students are more likely to remember concepts they discover on their own. Teachers have found that discovery learning is most successful when students have prerequisite knowledge and undergo some structured experiences.

Modern technology can now provide a virtual environment for students to explore. Medio's *Exploring Ancient Architecture* provides students with different ancient sites to explore for example, Stonehenge and an Egyptian pyramid. Students can 'walk' around the sites and explore places as they were when they were built. In

IVI Publishing's *Louis Cat Orze* students are immersed in a richly rendered, historically accurate model of Louis XIV's decadent court at Versailles during the year 1697. Students are challenged to solve the mystery of the queen's missing necklace.

The whimsical feline Louis Cat Orze guides users as they explore the ins and outs of the palace. The WWW can now link students to virtual worlds created using the vrml markup language.

Although the 'worlds' are fairly simplistic at this point the potential is there for virtual field trips to many educational places where students will be able to control the tour.

Simulations are another area where computer technology can support children's learning. Scholastic Software's *Operation Frog* aquaints students with the structure and components of a body system. It can take the place of dissection work with a real frog.

For many schools it is less expensive (since it can be done over and over), less offensive to students and more flexible. Many teachers find simulations offer effective supplements to real labs, either to prepare students for making good use of the actual labs, or a follow-ups with variations on the original experiments.

Maxis Software produces *SimCity*, it allows students to manipulate several factors while developing a community. This helps them focus on factors they must consider when developing a local project to benefit their community. As a final example, simulations can provide students with experiences that they could not do in real life. *Science Toolkit: Earthquake Module* by Broderbund allows students to cause an earthquake and observe its activities.

Postmodern Phenomenological Models

Action research

Action research is a reflective process of progressive problem solving lead by individuals working with others in teams or as part of a "community of practice" to improve the way they address issues and solve problems. Action research can also be undertaken by larger organisations or institutions, assisted or guided by professional researchers, with the aim of improving their strategies, practices, and knowledge of the environments within which they practice.

Action research is an iterative inquiry process that balances problem solving actions implemented in a collaborative context with data-driven collaborative analysis or research to understand underlying causes enabling future predictions about personal and organisational change. After six decades of action research development, many methodologies have evolved that adjust the balance to focus more on the actions taken or more on the research that results from the reflective understanding of the actions.

This tension exists between those that are more driven by the researcher's agenda to those more driven by participants; those that are motivated primarily by instrumental goal attainment to those motivated primarily by the aim of personal, organisational, or societal transformation; and 1st-, to 2nd-, to 3rd-person research (i.e. my research on my own action, aimed primarily at personal change; our research on our group (family/team), aimed primarily at improving the group; and 'scholarly' research aimed primarily at theoretical generalisation and/or large scale change).

Action research challenges traditional social science, by moving beyond reflective knowledge created by outside experts sampling variables to an active moment-to-moment theorising, data collecting, and inquiring occurring in the midst of emergent structure. "Knowledge is always gained through action and for action. From this starting point, to question the validity of social knowledge is to question, not how to develop a reflective science about action, but how to develop genuinely well-informed action—how to conduct an action science".

3

Reasonable Learning

When reason is held to be a strict adjudicator of legitimate and illegitimate expression, its effect is often to suppress those beliefs and values which do not measure up to its standards. This formalist conception of rationality has fallen under withering attack by current postmodern writers, especially those speaking from poststructuralist and/or feminist perspectives. The compelling elements of their critique, while questioning some of their conclusions.

First, as many postmodernists say, that there is something inherently discursive about any ordering system for thought. Invent or create the rules we choose to live by, through the ways that we speak and interact with one another. We do not discover them waiting, pristine and fully-formed, to be uncovered through the contemplations of pure reason. Over the course of our collective cultural history *we make them up*. This is true even for the conventions of argumentation themselves.

Although think, and act in ways that have become second nature to us, this is not evidence that they are universal or necessary for *all* legitimate speech, thought, and action. But the validity of this criticism does not yield the conclusion that all alternative forms of speech, thought, and action are equally good or in principle beyond comparison. There is *some* nonarbitrary reason why we think and act the way we do. When a particular way of adjudicating competing claims about truth, value, or proper course of action has been retained, developed, and refined over a long period of time, there must be something to recommend it beyond the preferences of a particular group that advocates it; it must be fulfilling a complex set of purposes, and its very persistence over time suggests a flexibility and efficacy that not all alternatives can match.

Second, the criticism that formal conceptions of rationality have excluded or denigrated considerations of affect and related noncognitive elements of thought and feeling, has merit. It is certainly true, at the level of social interaction, that an exaggerated bias toward a formal, impersonal way of expressing or justifying ideas has in fact excluded or disadvantaged potential participants (especially women and certain ethnic and racial groups) from the discussion that is — or should be — an open society. Beyond this, it can be argued persuasively that the actual *substance* of our beliefs and values has been distorted as a result; the clearest case for this, has been in the area of ethics, where feminist authors such as Carol Gilligan and Nel Noddings have pointed out that modes of understanding and judgment more typical of women have been neglected by traditional accounts of moral reasoning, to the *disadvantage* of our appreciation of the range of moral understandings and sentiments.

An equally telling argument can be framed for the inclusion of affective and noncognitive elements in the dynamics of reasoning generally; for if reason has a discursive or communicative grounding, then part of the process of creating and maintaining effective communicative relations will entail matters of feeling, empathy, and concern. But arguing for a more inclusive and multifaceted conception of reason is not the same thing as abandoning the value of any sort of reasonable standards. On the contrary, it is to *reinforce* the value of standards, because the very values of tolerance and openness to diversity of modes of thought and feeling express such standards.

Third, there is a valid core to the concern that the presumed neutrality and universality of a particular style of rational thought and speech typical of modern, Western cultures has been taken as the essential node toward which all other cultures must converge. There does seem to be a kind of cultural imperialism at work here. But the very capacity of "Third World" critics to identify, comprehend, question, and reject certain forms of Western thought has itself been facilitated by some features of that very mode of thought. This suggests that they are, if not necessary and unavoidable, at least *difficult* to avoid; and it certainly should give pause to the assertion that they are entirely pernicious.

Fourth, Richard Rorty and other neopragmatists are correct that considerations of context and purpose are intrinsic to the determination of what it is reasonable to do, and that a significant shortcoming of the formal conception of rationality has been the presumption that one can deduce, a priori, conclusions that will be compelling or true across all circumstances. This false universalism underestimates the extent to which reasoning is a situated human achievement, undertaken within communities of inquiry and conversation. But it would be a mistake to assume that this requires that what any such communities might happen to conclude are equally valid, that there is no way to compare them, or that in practice certain conclusions cannot come to be shared by most or all. It is simply to say that when this happens, it is not because they have arrived at the same ineluctable "truths." It is not surprising, after all, that human groups, confronted with similar questions or problems, will often arrive at similar or comparable conclusions; nor is it surprising that some can accept or learn from those of others.

"Reasonableness" refers to the dispositions and capacities of a certain kind of person, a person who is related in specific contexts to other persons — not to the following of formal rules and procedures of thought. A common trend, for example, in much current writing on critical thinking is to suggest the limitations of "logicality" as an approximation of what a critical thinker is and does; rather, we need to supplement the skills of logical reasoning with dispositions to apply them in contexts of practice. In some cases, unfortunately, the characterization of these dispositions is rather thin: the difference between the logical rule "always test a syllogism for valid structure" and the "disposition to test syllogisms for valid structure" is hardly worth talking about.

Similarly, the "rational passions" discussed by Israel Scheffler and others, such as a passion for rigor and clarity, are sometimes little more than the rephrasing of formal criteria in an emotive language. For this reason, along with others, the term "virtues" to "dispositions." Virtues are flexible aspects of character, expressed out of our sense of self and integrity, but also fostered and encouraged by the communities and relations with others that provide the context in which we choose and act. The term "disposition" does little to suggest this richness and complexity.

A stronger characterization of reasonableness as a human characteristic and achievement requires, first of all, a much deeper conception of how virtues affect conduct: they are not simply the activating sentiments that motivate us to apply the formal rules we have learned, but the aspects of character that bring us to care about learning or paying attention to such criteria in the first place. They are part of who we are. A person who is reasonable wants to make sense, wants to be fair to alternative points of view, wants to be careful and prudent in the adoption of important positions in life, is willing to admit when he or she has made a mistake, and so on; and these qualities are not exhibited simply by following certain formal rules of reasoning.

They are enormously more complex than that, since they are manifested in a broad range of situations that are not governed by such formal rules. Because they are more basic and extensive than any set of rules, these virtues might even be manifested in specific situations by ignoring some of these rules (as when someone violates the norm of strict precision and accuracy in trying to express a simple idea to a child). In this view, it is because persons are reasonable, or want to be, that they should concern themselves with "logicality" as a useful heuristic for ordered thought.

The second and related dimension of reasonableness concerns the capacity to enter into the types of communicative relations in which persons together inquire, disagree, adjudicate, explain, or argue their views in the pursuit of a reasonable outcome (that is, an outcome that reasonable people are satisfied with). The dispositions of reasonableness described above are manifested in the ways that persons speak with and listen to one another. This communicative aspect is chiefly what makes the pursuit and attainment of reasoned positions a *practical* and *contextual* endeavor. The apparent circularity of saying that reasonable people pursue understandings in a particular way, and that a reasonable conclusion to such deliberations is simply what the persons involved settle upon, is less a circle than a back-and-forth feedback process. The adequacy of our reasoning and conversation by the efficacy and social acceptability of the conclusions they derive; the reliability of our conclusions by the thoroughness and care of the processes by which we reached them.

What makes this a substantive conception, then, is that the outcome of a given line of inquiry often cannot be settled conclusively in advance or inferred by tracing out a particular logical argument; rather, the process of reasoned inquiry is manifested in the thoughts, conversations, and choices that the actual persons involved pursue toward some conclusion — and if they are reasonable people, this conclusion is as reliable as any can be.

Of course, that conclusion might be mistaken, but it can be recognized as such and rectified only through a further extension of the same process. The epistemic dimension of reasonableness is thereby inverted: the question is no longer, "What procedures of inquiry or argument are most likely to yield the Truth?" but rather, "When people have sought to understand the truth of their situation, what are the general patterns of investigation that they have settled upon over time?"

Among these patterns of investigation, the rules of logic or scientific inquiry play an important but limited part, because they are effective as such only in social contexts of communication, practice, and judgment. The difficult question, then, concerns the nature of these contexts, and how we conduct ourselves in them; in a short essay I can only sketch an answer. My strategy is to select four traits that seem central to reasonableness (objectivity, fallibilism, pragmatism, and judgment), and to show how they can be translated from a formal, decontextualized language to one concerned with personal character, practical contexts, and communicative relations. These characteristics are both richer and more effective when we understand them in this way; that they are better able to withstand some of the postmodern criticisms discussed earlier; and that they lead more directly to educational projects.

Being objective

What, in fact, is necessary in order for a person to adopt an objective standpoint? Two conditions appear crucial. The first is an attitude of tolerance, the capacity to regard alternative positions without a "rush to judgment." An objective person is one who can withhold his or her own opinions in an engagement with other points of view. This capacity is fostered, not primarily by the exercise of certain intellectual skills, but by the exercise of a demeanor and capacity for restraint.

There are many other aspects of tolerance as well: being able to recognize what one's own biases might be, acknowledging the limits of one's capacity to appreciate fully the viewpoints of others, or caring enough about others to exert the effort necessary to hear and comprehend what they are saying. My point here is that lacking such characteristics, a person cannot enact that component of reasonableness we call "objectivity." And the acquisition and exercise of these characteristics is clearly not a purely cognitive/rational endeavor. On the contrary, it has nothing to do with a lack of commitment, caring, or feeling.

Nor is the acquisition and expression of this virtue an individual achievement. Developing tolerance, for example, depends upon the kinds of communicative and other social interactions one has had with others throughout the course of one's life. Moreover, viewing these capacities in the context of real human interactions also helps make clear when tolerance might *not* be a reasonable response: when one has reached the limits of one's capacities to be detached, or when certain points of view are so repugnant that it is unrealistic and unreasonable to expect one's self not to judge them.

Being objective requires a pluralistic sentiment. Objectivity is supported, not by the position of holding no view, but by the position of having regarded enough other views thoughtfully and sympathetically to realize that each has something to be said for it, so that one is distanced somewhat from the attitude that there is or can be one "best" way of all. This pluralism is fostered, of course, partly by having been exposed to a sufficient range of differences, but also by engaging them in some process of give-and-take that has enabled one to consider seriously the merits of each. This, it seems to me, is a chief talent of persons whom we consider to be "objective" — and it is, a fundamentally different analysis of that virtue than those normally found in the literature.

What this line of argument suggests is that in the pursuits of objectivity, values such as tolerance and pluralism are *methodological* as well as *moral* edicts. Our thinking will be richer, more balanced, and more fair when we are able to hear and consider a variety of alternatives. Being able to do so requires not only some intellectual capacities, but also aspects of character, personal relations, and social contexts that encourage and support the development of this virtue. We all know persons who have great intellect but who cannot detach their critical capacities sufficiently to hear and consider alternative points of view. To that degree, they lack objectivity. Similarly, persons who can listen to anything and not react critically to it seem to lack a kind of discernment.

Accepting Fallibilism

One of the great aphorisms of modern philosophy is Karl Popper's reminder not to be afraid of making mistakes, because it is only through the discovery of error, through some process of falsification, that we are driven to change. Indeed, Popper's recommendation seems to extend far beyond the confines of scientific hypothesis testing, where it is typically applied, to a broader vision and attitude toward life.

In a variety of contexts, both personal and professional, intellectual and emotional, we all have experience with failure, error, and disappointment. If we can live with these, as we must, it is usually with the understanding that they have formed us, taught us something, strengthened our capacity to endure change. In this broader sense, the acceptance of fallibilism is a component of a reasonable character.

What is involved in this virtue? First of all, it requires us to make certain commitments, or take certain risks, that run the possibility of error. Purposely hiding behind obscurantism, withholding commitment, or playing it safe by only conforming to the conventional and obvious, are all ways of avoiding mistakes — and hence, ultimately, of avoiding learning and change. Second, it requires a capacity to recognize that one is wrong, which is fundamentally linked with the capacity to *admit* (to oneself and to others) that one was wrong. This includes our capacity to hear and respond thoughtfully to the criticisms of others. Third, it involves a capacity for reflection, as we ponder not only that we *have* made a mistake, but also why it happened and how we can change to avoid repeating it in the future.

Once again, we know individuals who have all the intellectual skills one could admire, but who find it difficult to acknowledge error. This is a defect from the standpoint of a reasonable character. However, it would be a mistake to regard this entirely as a shortcoming of the individual, and not as a breakdown in a broader developmental context that implicitly and often explicitly rewards unreasonable conduct.

Sometimes it is dangerous to admit error, and sometimes the damage done to personal relations or self-esteem make admission of one's mistakes a punishable offense. In the university context, for example, the rise of an adversarial method as the primary model of academic engagement frequently rewards those who are most vigorous in defending their own point of view and attacking those of others.

The give-and-take of criticism within communities of inquiry is illegitimate; on the contrary, it is a crucial process in a culture that recognizes fallibilism as the pivot point of change. But when this process takes place in a system of "high stakes" rewards and punishments; when certain aggressive aspects of personality and verbal style are falsely taken to be proxies for a healthy critical process; when the pressures and power relations of such contexts are such that certain prospective participants are intimidated from entering the conversation, then we mistake the *forms* of debate and critical interaction for the *substance* of carefully and sympathetically comparing the merits of a range of points of view and subjecting them to some process of thoughtful scrutiny and revision. We should not be surprised in these contexts when people have developed a razor-sharp capacity to dissect the ideas of others but a stultified capacity to alter or abandon their own presuppositions.

Reasonableness, on this view, expresses a capacity for change, a change prompted by one's own recognition and acknowledgment of error, but also supported by a social environment in which this process is regarded with favor, not disdain. "Falsifiability" is normally taken in the literature to be a description of the characteristics and history of a theory or research program; but it includes more than this, since theories are held by persons and because research programs comprise individuals with various personal, institutional, and (often) financial interests in maintaining and perpetuating their positions. Hence "falsifiability," and conceptual change as a result, are achievable not only because of the features of a particular intellectual framework, but because of the capacities for facing up to and responding to error on the part of those who hold it.

Embracing Pragmatism

Most important purposes , it reflects a tolerance for uncertainty, imperfection, and incompleteness as the existential conditions of human thought, value, or action, yet also recognizes the need for persistence and flexibility in confronting such difficulties.

A reasonable person is frequently in situations where insufficient information is available, where problems appear intractable, where outcomes are unpredictable. Here, most of all, we see his or her capacities tested. We expect people to be reasonable in contexts and activities with which they are familiar, and where they are confident; the threats to reasonableness are when conventional responses fail, when doubts prevail. In such difficulties, what makes the responses of a person reasoned and reliable is whether he or she can approach the present problems with an open mind, a willingness and capacity to adapt, and persistence in the face of initial failure or confusion.

In this case, these capacities operate at a much deeper and more pervasive level than any particular set of skills or strategies — although, certainly, having some appropriate skills, having experience with similar situations, and having some track record of success in coping with them are also relevant to whether a person will respond constructively to a new challenge.

Also supportive of such capacities are social contexts in which an emphasis on success is not exaggerated; in which failure or frustration are accepted as inevitable conditions of growth; and in which offering cooperative assistance and constructive suggestions — or asking for them — are socially and personally acceptable options. Once again, this provides a quite different characterization of the person who is reasonable and of the type of context that fosters and supports reasonable conduct.

EXERCISING JUDGMENT

One of the reasons that a dispositional account of reasonableness is prior to, and not just a supplement for, an emphasis on "logicality" is that one of the chief characteristics of a reasonable person is the ability to judge, to distinguish situations in which a rational calculation in the narrow sense might be called for, and when it is not.We need to build into the concept of reasonableness an awareness of its own limitations: that a reasonable person is one who knows when *not* to try to figure certain things out in a particular rational way, and who regards the skills of rationality and the assessment of reasons as simply heuristics in the much more complex process of trying to decide what to believe and what to do — heuristics that can help guide our choices, but not govern them.

It is not reasonable to try to apply the analysis of logic, or the strict rules of evidence, or the critique of informal fallacies, to each and every situation; we would react very peculiarly to someone who did (this is the perennial joke about Mr. Spock on *Star Trek*, of course).

Part of judgment, as well, is a capacity for prudence and moderation, even in the exercise of reason itself. We are not always reasonable; we occasionally fail to act upon our own best inclinations; we frequently fall short of our aspirations. Acknowledging and accepting this in ourselves, and in those around us, and asking others to accept it in us, is related to the acceptance of fallibilism and the willingness to embrace imperfection and incompleteness that the pragmatic spirit; it is the recognition of the patterns of grey-on-grey that typically background human choice and action. There is often more than one reasonable thing to believe, to say, or to do; and it is part of the fallacy of formalistic conceptions of rationality that they seek a determinative calculus that will converge on the one "best" or "right" answer.

The key virtues are a capacity to hold competing considerations in balance, and to accept tensions and uncertainty as the conditions of serious reflection. Such broad capacities as paying attention to "relevant" information, respecting complexities and uncertainties, keeping an open mind to alternative points of view, and appreciating the limitations of one's tools of inquiry as well as their utility, are not *formal* capacities — yet without exercising such judgments, we cannot be reasonable in any full sense of the term.

Related to this point, our attainment of reasonableness is a matter of degree: some times we are more reasonable than others; around some people we are more reasonable. Our aspiration is not to cross some ultimate barrier from the "irrational" to the "rational," but to improve, through a process of learning and development, our capacities to be reasonable, and those of others with whom we interact. This awareness should *increase* our sense of interdependence and kinship with others, and provide a healthy counterbalance to the smug confidence that we can answer every question, solve every problem, or resolve every dilemma on our own.

Finally, those whom we respect as reasonable are judicious about when and how they follow the dictates of argument in the strict sense of the term, and they are receptive to the influence of other kinds of persuasion as well. In the actual practice of human communication, strict and conclusive argument are very rare; alongside that is an enormous range of interlocutory styles, including questions, allusions, unsubstantiated suggestions, metaphors, and other tropes, as well as an even broader range of expressions, gestures, touches, musical sounds, and other kinds of communication.

The capacity of all these sorts of utterances to move us is "extra-rational" only in a very narrow sense of that term. When we endeavor to be reasonable in social contexts of interaction, this entails remaining open to the influences of other avenues of mutual exploration, negotiation, and the pursuit of understanding. In this endeavor, a respect for the force of reasons is crucial, as is the attempt to be clear, coherent, and accurate in what one says. But it is not everything.

In a fuller argument, how this characterization of being reasonable avoids the postmodern criticisms summarized at the start of this essay. But the outlines of a response are fairly clear. Conceiving of reasonableness as a set of virtues does not commit us to a belief in a master narrative or a pure meta-discourse; on the contrary, characterizing reason as a concrete, imperfect, human attainment responds sympathetically to the criticism that rationality has been abstracted from the field of human interrelationships and politics. The elements of objectivity, fallibilism, pragmatism, and judgment each can be explored in ways that do justice to the diversity of human thoughts, values, and forms of life, without falling into a relativism that is unable to recommend or criticize any manner of thinking about the complexities and ambiguities of human existence. While being flexible enough to accommodate a broad range of human processes of communication, investigation, or negotiation, these four elements also provide a basis for excluding others that can be shown to be counterproductive to intelligent, committed, and caring thought and action.

It is the hallmark of a reasonable person to be able to consider a range of worthy possibilities, and to acknowledge the potential benefits inherent in each, without becoming incapable of choosing or judging between them (while acknowledging at the same time that others might legitimately choose *from among that range* differently).

Finally, this conception of reasoning has an essential *educational* element, not only because of the general problem of how to foster and encourage these characteristics in new learners, but because the conception requires an educational process at the level of its very definition and justification. In each of the four elements , fallibilism, pragmatism, and judgment — the process by which we exercise and cultivate these virtues involves us in a set of communicative interactions (i.e., educative interactions) with others. They are neither acquired nor exercised in isolation.

Reasonableness is an educational aim because it is bound to and illuminates fundamental aspects of how the process of education itself occurs: through encountering new, challenging, and often conflicting ideas; through making mistakes and trying to learn from them; through persisting through levels of difficulty and discouragement to something new and worthwhile; and through learning to judge in practice both the applicability and the limits of the general principles and skills one acquires. Each of these, in turn, depends upon a range of communicative and other relations the learner forms with other people; objectivity, fallibilism, pragmatism, and judgment ought to be conceived as *social,* as well as individual, attainments. Through the exercise of these we *learn to be reasonable.*

4

Psychological Development of Child

The child can only live his childhood; to understand childhood is the province of the adult. But whose vantage point is to prevail, the adult's or the child? The adult recognizes differences between himself and a child. But these differences are usually reduced to the quantitative, to a matter of mere degree.

When he compare himself with a child, an adult sees the child as relatively or eve totally incapable of actions or tasks he himself can accomplish. These inabilities can shed light on differences in mental organization between the child and the adult.

An adult demonstrates his egocentrism through his conviction that all mental development must naturally and inevitably lead to modes of thought and feeling exactly like his own and bearing the particular stamp of the time and place in which he lives. If he does somehow manage to achieve the insight that a child's thoughts an feelings do follow paths quite different from his own, it does not occur to him to consider this as anything more than an oddity.

Since this oddity is constant and seems as necessary and normal as his own ideological system, he feels an attempt should certainly be made to understand its mechanism. But he first finds he must understand the nature of this oddity. Is it true that the mentality of the child and that of the adult follow different paths and conform to different principles; that the transition from one to the other involves a total transformation; that the principles the adult believes govern his own thought constitute an immutable and inflexible norm in the light of which a child's thought may be dismissed as outside the domain of reason; and that the intellectual inferences of a child bear no relation whatever to an adult's? Could adult intelligence have remained so rich and productive if it really had been forced to abandon the sources from which the child's intelligence springs?

After all, it is the world of adults that the environment imposes on the child, so that at each stage the structures and contents of the mind display a certain uniformity. But it does not follow that the adult need take into account only those aspects of a child's thought that the adult imposes. Even the manner in which a child assimilates material may bear absolutely no resemblance to the way an adult utilizes it. If the adult surpasses the child, the child in his way surpasses the adult.

The child's frequent inability to use a previously acquired skill has been pointed out by several authors. The explanations given by W. Stern and, later, by Piaget are more or less similar. A particular mental operation extends over different levels, and during the course of mental development the passage from one level to the next always occurs in the same sequence. The circumstances under which an operation must be carried out present obstacles of widely varying difficulty. If the difficulty increases, the operation may then be performed at a lower level. Thus, the same person, at the same age, can perform the same operation at a variety of levels. Piaget, by way of explanation, uses concepts such as causality, which the child seems to know how to apply objectively to everyday activity, though in his explanations at the "verbal level" he regresses to much more subjective forms of causality, such as voluntaristic or affective ones.

Although a child's mental development presupposes a kind of network in which internal and external factors are intertwined, it is possible to unravel their distinct, respective roles. The internal factors are presumably responsible for the strict sequence of developmental phases, the chief determinant of which is the growth of the organs. Substances of relatively simple chemical composition seem to perform the decisive roles of stimulating and regulating the differentiation of organs. This differentiation sets the stage for the emergence of the future organism's structures from the embryo (in which they are latent, though invisible). These substances are the hormones, secreted by the endocrine glands.

Each hormone is endowed with a strict specificity, although hormones are often mutually dependent. They control the appearance and development of different kinds of tissues, and the sequence in which they are activated is precisely attuned to the needs of growth. In addition to their morphogenic role, they also exercise an equally specific elective action on physiological and mental functions. Von Monakow regarded them as the material substrate of the instincts.

The problem of the relations between functional maturation and functional learning now arises. Obviously, to systematically impute every development to the maturation of the corresponding organs would be only to repeat, in modified form, the old explanations in which every effect was merely referred to an entity modeled after it. But to contend a priori, as Piaget does in his book La naissance de l'intelligence chez l'enf ant, that during the course of mental development new activities emerge that must necessarily have their source in the functional activation of matured organic structure, is to mistake a simple description, however rich, penetrating, and ingenious, for the deep-seated mechanisms of mental life.

Importance of Play

It has been said that play is the activity uniquely appropriate to the child; and as a child often sees deeply engrossed in his play, certain authors have felt obliged to attribute to children what they call serious games. According to Charlotte Bühler, play is a stage in the total development of the child that disappears of its own accord at succeeding periods. Indeed, play is mingled in all of the child's activity so long as that activity remains spontaneous and untouched by objects introduced for educative purposes. At the beginning, games are purely functional; then come games of make-believe and games of practical skill.

In his play the child repeats the impressions of events he has just experienced. He reproduces; he imitates. For the very young child, imitation is the only rule of the game so long as he is unable to go beyond the concrete, living model to abstract instructions. Initially, children's comprehension is no more than the assimilation of others to themselves and themselves to others, and in this process imitation plays an important role.

Imitation, as the instrument of this fusion, demonstrates a contradiction that explains certain contrasts on which play thrives. Imitation is not random; the child is very selective. He imitates people who enjoy the most prestige in his own eyes, those who evoke his positive, affectionate feelings. At the same time, the child "borrows" or becomes these persons. Always totally immersed in what he is doing, he accordingly imagines and wishes himself to be them. But soon his latent awareness of this borrowing arouses in him feelings of hostility against the person serving as a model, whom he cannot eliminate. He finally comes to resent this person whose absolutely incontestable and frustrating superiority he often continues to experience.

Between the ages of six and seven it becomes possible to disengage the child from his spontaneous activity and to divert his interest to others. Until comparatively recently, productive labor, including factory work, began at this age. Indeed, in some colonial countries this is still the case. In France, the child enters school at this age and tackles the demands of formal education—which include self-discipline.

Two contradictory elements are basic to all imitation. One is a plastic union in which the external impression is taken in and then discharged again gently from its strange receptacle, leaving only those elements that are able to be incorporated into existing mental structures. The result is a new, albeit rudimentary, capacity. The second and active aspect, equally important to the first, is execution and completion. The ensuing act requires tentative, and sometimes obvious, gropings. Separation and recombination of suitable elements are operations whose often long-enduring imperfections indicate the difficulties these processes involve.

In particular, the rediscovered gestures and movements may not yet be in the right order. Taken by themselves they by no means reproduce the model; they must conform to the requirements of an internal prototype. However, as they become more explicit, they make possible and even encourage objective comparisons with the external model. Alternation between these two contrary but complementary phases of intuitive assimilation and controlled execution may then assume a more or less rapid cadence until the imitation appears adequate.

Child Development Functions

Emotions, affectivity's outward expression, trigger changes that tend to reduce the emotions themselves. Emotions are the underlying basis for the gregarious drives that constitute a rudimentary form of communication and community. The relations made possible through emotions create finer and more subtle forms of expression and transform these into more and more specialized instruments of social interaction. But as their significance becomes more precisely defined, these modes of expression become more autonomous and detached from emotion.

Instead of releasing the floodtide of emotion, they tend to dam up emotion and compartmentalize it, thus destroying its pervasiveness and power of contagion. As soon as speech and convention become the media of mimicry, convention multiplies nuances, tacit understandings, and innuendos. Subtlety is thus introduced, in contrast to the undivided expression of pure emotion.

Emotion and intellectual activity follow the same evolution and present the same antagonism. Even before a situation is analyzed the activities that a situation provokes and the dispositions and attitudes it arouses give it meaning. In mental development this practical insight appears long before the ability to discriminate and compare. It is a first form of comprehension, wholly dominated by the interest of the moment and thoroughly absorbed in the particular. The sharing of attitudes is the first crude form of mutual contact or understanding between individuals, even though it is still totally engrossed in desires or impulses of the moment.

An image that is useful for comparison or expectation can emerge from these pragmatic and concrete relations only by gradully reducing the role of body reactions—that is, of emotions and affectivity. Conversely, each time that affective attitudes and the corresponding emotion again become dominant, an image loses its richness, becomes blurred, and vanishes. This phenomenon is commonly observed in adults: suppression of emotion through intellectual control or by simple translation of its motives or conditions into intellectual modes; or, on the other hand, the routing of reason and objective representations by emotion. In the child, progress from purely casual, personal, and emotional reactions to a more stable conception of things is a slow process. Regression is very frequent.

In the domain of affectivity, this conflict produces transformations. If rationalist theories of emotion have seemed plausible, it is by virtue of the importance of intellectual motives and images in the realm of feelings and passion. In reality there is a transfer between emotion and the latter feelings. This tranfer is dependent on the age of the child. But the most emotional children do not necessarily become the most sentimental or the most passionate. Rather, it is a question of different types of children, in whom the various psychic functions are balanced differently.

Role of Language

The beginnings of speech in the child coincide with marked progress in his practical skills. In this respect, a comparison of the child's behavior with that of the monkey is particularly striking. Thus, Boutan, followed by others, particularly Kellog and his wife, compared a child in the preverbal and verbal period with a young monkey in identical situations. Child and monkey were even raised together in the same environment. During the initial period, behavior was very similar. But as soon as the child acquired the use of speech he rapidly outstripped his companion. For example, when presented with several boxes arranged in a row, one of which contained a treat, the training necessary to find the special box without error at first yielded similar results. But if the order of the boxes was altered, the monkey became perplexed and had to rely on trial and error, whereas the child, once he could speak, was quickly able to discover the change.

Obviously, speech was still at a level too primitive to warrant the hypothesis of an internal instruction or some sort of mental calculation. Rather, the child was displaying a capacity to imagine a displacement, a line, or a direction that did not exist between the objects perceived. This capacity is possible only if vision, instead of being total absorption in the objects themselves, deploys them over an imaginary canvas of stable and interdependent positions.

Without this ability, there is no way to conceptualize any sort of order or to mentally construct a sequence. This capacity is also necessary to give order to the successive parts of discourse. The loss of one of these abilities entails the loss of the other. An aphasic cannot indicate the directions up, down, right, left, etc., with his eyes closed. When his eyes are open, that which he points out, according to Sieckmann, is not a direction, but an object—for example, the ceiling, the floor, the hand holding the razor, the hand that is not writing, etc.

A necessary but not sufficient condition is the awareness that objects and movements are seen successively or in transition. This by no means explains all the functions of language, nor its important implications for the species and the individual. Without going into the social relations made possible by, and patterned after, language, or into the fact that each dialect is a bearer and transmitter of history, one may at least state that it is language that has transformed into consciousness the compact mélange of things and actions that constitute the raw material of experience. Actually, language is not the cause of thought; it is the indispensable tool and sustaining element in thought's progress. If one sometimes falls behind the other, their reciprocal action quickly reestablishes a harmonious balance.

Through language, the object of thought need no longer be confined to things presently perceived. Language provides a means whereby the representation of things no longer present, or of things that might appear, can be evoked and compared and contrasted between themselves and with current perceptions. In reintegrating the absent into the present, language provides a means of expressing, fixing, and analyzing the present. It imposes the world of signs, the marks of thought, on direct experience, in circumstances in which thought can imagine and pursue a free course, unite what was disjointed, and separate what had been simultaneous. But this substitution of the sign for the thing is not without its problems and pitfalls. It forces the practical solution of problems that can be dealt with only later through speculative reflection.

In clarifying what was unclear and permanently establishing what was transitory, representational thought, delimited by means of signs, gives rise to an opposition between the same and the other, the like and the unlike, the one and the many, the permanent and the transitory, the identical and the changing, the stationary and the moving, and the being and the becoming. Many inconsistencies and incongruities that startle us in a child have their actual source in the clash between these contradictory notions, however adept the child may be at evasion through omission or at circumvention with the aid of speech and thinking habits acquired from adults. The advance that language permits thought to make and the effort it demands from thought in return may be clearly seen in the setback thought suffers when language appears to regress—as in aphasics.

Discontinuity in Development

The discontinuity in the thought of the child has another cause whose consequences are no less significant: the inadequacy of accommodation to an object, whether it activates motor, perceptual, or intellectual mechanisms. Accommodation long remains hesitant and irresolute. It oscillates back and forth around its object, its precise focus remains elusive, and its fluctuations are out of step with those of its objective.

Like a kitten that on seeing its ball of yarn disappear into an inaccessible place stops short and becomes uncertain, the most lively and playful child has his moments of sudden disorientation and loss of objective. The moment the object of his thought eludes him, a faintly bewildered expression passes over his face. Thus, a fluctuating image of things results, making it difficult to identify any one object and easy to confuse one with another. The notion of possible transformations of things, far from being diminished through contact with reality, instead finds its base in this contact. Hence, the phantasmagorias a child finds so believable should cause us no surprise.

The initial lack of distinction between the self and others implies inadequate discrimination of others. When a small child pursues every man he sees with the name "Daddy," it would be premature to say that he identifies them all with his father or that he puts them into a class denoted by the name of the individual because he does not know the collective name for them. He experiences a reaction to the whole, which evokes by means of certain of its features a specific quality in which the parts are confused with the whole and hence are liable to entail a confusion of totalities otherwise mutually distinct.

Development Stages

The first weeks of life are totally taken up by the needs of sleep and nourishment. However, turgescence of the genitals has been observed during the days immediately following birth. In the girl infant it may even reach the point of blood loss. Although it appears to be the result of hormones, the mechanism and significance of this turgescence are still imperfectly understood. The act of feeding involves a child's first organized movements. But the gesticulations elicited from the infant by a diaper change or a bath exceed the narrow limits of this first field of movement. A detailed record of these movements will reveal two tendencies.

On the one hand, there is a disappearance of certain spontaneous or elicited reactions, which are reabsorbed or inhibited by less automatic activities. On the other hand, there is an emergence of new gestures often derived from dissociation of global muscular actions and exhibiting a tendency to integrate fragments sequentially: From the third month on, these advances in movement become the child's major occupation.

The infant's first affective manifestations are limited to cries of hunger or colic or to the calm of sleep or digestion. Their differentiation is initially very slow. But by the age of six months, the structured channels available to the infant for expressing his emotions are sufficiently diversified to serve as a broad osmotic surface with his human environment. This is a major stage in his mental development. His gestures acquire a certain efficacy through the mediation of other persons, and the gestures and movements of others take on specific anticipatory meanings. However, this reciprocity is at first completely undifferentiated. It involves the child's total participation, whereas at a later stage he will come to define himself, already profoundly enriched by this initial absorption in others. A synchronism is to be noted at this stage, as the child also begins to show an interest in colors at the age of six months.

During the latter third of the first year, sensorimotor action patterns begin to be systematized and become the means by which movements may be linked with their perceptual effects. Proprioceptive and sensorial impressions become mutually attuned, down to their subtlest nuances. After first establishing a continuity and concordance among their variations over extended sequences, these impressions can then go on to mutual exploration and discovery.

The voice refines the ear; the ear cultivates the voice. Sounds, which become identifiable and discernible through this concurrence of various impressions, can later be recognized when they come from an external source. When the child visually follows the intricate patterns and contours traced by his own moving hand, he is marking out the first spatial references of his visual field. Thus marked out by proprioceptive responsiveness, the perceptual fields may then merge and in so doing eliminate their source or, rather, consign it to anonymity, the source now having superseded interoceptive or visceral responsiveness. The same object becomes identifiable in different perceptual fields, and their fused totality acquires sufficiently real attributes for the child to seek in it an object that has disappeared or that has been revealed through data from only one of the senses.

But walking, and then language, which develop

during the second year, once again come to upset this delicate balance in behavior. Objects that a child is able to fetch and carry from place to place and that he knows have a name become dissociated from their settings and are manipulated for their own sake. He picks them up, pushes them, drags them, moves them about by hand or in a cart; he arranges them in piles, either at random or by kind; he empties and fills boxes and bags. But at another level, the independence achieved by the child through this ability to get about by himself and the greater diversity that language introduces into his relations with others around him make possible a more resolute and clear cut affirmation of his personality. The crises of opposition, and then of imitation, begin at the age of three and last until age five.

During the period in which he is intent upon appearing distinct from others, the child also becomes increasingly capable of distinguishing between objects and sorting them by color, shape, dimensions, tactile qualities, and odor. At the age of four a child begins to be concerned with, and self-conscious about, his attitudes and manners, what they are, and how they may appear. He begins to blush when embarrassed, which conversely allows him the material for mockery and jesting. Grimaces, jokes, and pranks delight him. He enjoys laughing and seeing himself laugh. His name, surname, age, and home become for him an image of his diminutive person, which, in turn, becomes for him a sort of sounding board for his own thought.

Now that he is able to observe himself, he diffuses his attention less and pursues a task with more patience and perseverance. He contemplates himself in his works and deeds and becomes attached to things he has made. He reflects upon them in his thoughts, along with himself, for comparison and contrast. Emulation is born, and with it the first needs for companionship. However, the groups that form are still of the gregarious type, in which each member takes his place spontaneously as follower or leader. But by this time the child no longer limits himself to the elaboration of further nuances in his discrimination of objects and their qualities: his perception becomes more abstract; and he begins to distinguish among patterns, lines, directions, positions, and graphic signs. Yet the actual observation of things, in which detail must be continually referred to the whole, the many to the one, and the variable to the constant for orientation, is still beyond his capacities.

After five years, school age begins; henceforth, interest will pass beyond the self to become involved with things. However, the transition is slow and difficult. Until the age of six or more, the child remains absorbed in his interests and activities of the moment. His activity has a certain exclusivity. He is unable to shuttle rapidly from object to object or from task to task. In order to divert her young pupils' attention from what they were doing to a proposed new object of attention, one teacher hit on the idea of an automatic interruptive gesture, which the child executed whenever she gave the signal.

School demands that intellectual activities be immediately concentrated on command, on subject matters that are consecutively and arbitrarily diverse. Schools have often abused this authority. The tasks imposed must to some extent tear the child away from his spontaneous interests, and too often these tasks are able to obtain from him only a constrained effort, a feigned attention, or simply intellectual apathy. Too often they are exercises with only a future usefulness, which is not at all apparent to the child executing them. Thus, it has seemed necessary to shore up the child's activity with accessory incentives. This is the purpose of rewards and punishments, which in many cases are still based on the principle of "the carrot or the stick"—that is, a simple technique of discipline and training. At the other extreme are those who claim to base the compulsory activities of the child on his sense of responsibility. The first method is inhibiting; the second, premature.

A trained animal responds to a cue with movements in accordance with inculcated sets of associations. It does not perform a task, which requires pursuit of an end, adjustment of means, rules to be observed, and sustained application of effort. But as the child is successively absorbed in each of his tasks, he seems no more capable than an animal of sustaining the burden of his tasks solely on the basis of his own independently conceived idea of what he owes himself. To appeal prematurely to this sense of obligation is to outline its features, so that far from promoting self-sufficiency, such an appeal imposes on a child a forced, confusedly understood dependence.

The period from seven to about twelve or fourteen years is the age at which syncretism yields to objectivity. Things and the self gradually lose their quality of being fragments of an absolute, undivided experience that impose themselves successively on intuition. The various categories of understanding bring to bear the most variegated array of classifications and relations. But the real initiator of these processes is the child's own activity, which itself enters into a categorical phase; it must now establish tasks and learn to apportion time to them so that each may be carried out with full possible effectiveness. Interest in a task is indispensable—far more important than simple training; it may suffice, and it precedes by far a constant and conscientious personal involvement in carrying out a task.

The taste a child acquires for things is commensurate with his desire and power to manage, modify, and transform them. He continually finds himself occupied with tearing down and building up. In this way he discovers the details, relations, and varied possibilities of things. He also selects his companions with a view toward determinate tasks. His preferences change according to the game or task. Naturally, he has regular companions, but all their interactions refer to their common ventures. They are united as collaborators or accomplices around mutual projects and mutual problems. They vie with each other through emulation in the execution of a task. Their projects determine their rivalries. Differences thus emerge in relationships, from which each child derives a notion of his own distinctness, according to circumstances, and at the same time, of his own essential continuity and individuality throughout a diversity of situations.

When friendship and rivalries are no longer based on agreement or conflict or interest in ongoing or impending tasks, when their justification is sought in moral affinities or moral repulsions, and when they seem to be concerned more with intimacy than with effective collaborations or conflicts, then childhood is already being undermined by puberty. Once again, the effects of the new period will permeate simultaneously all spheres of mental life. A single mood of discord or disquiet will make itself felt in actions, personal conduct, and cognitive processes. In each sphere, there are mysteries to penetrate. There is a continuing and undifferentiated need for possession, a need that is, in a certain sense, so basic that actual possession is unable to satisfy it and must go in quest of uncharted horizons.

From one stage to another, a child's mental development demonstrates that beyond the complexity of factors and functions and the variety and contrasts of the crises that punctuate it, there is a certain unity, an interrelatedness, both within each stage and across stages. To treat the child fragmentarily is contrary to nature. At each age he constitutes an indivisible and original whole.

In the succession of different periods, he remains one and the same being undergoing metamorphoses. Composed as he is of contrasts and conflicts, his whole self will only be that much more capable of further enrichment.

Stages in the Mental Development of Children

The problem of stages in the mental development of the child is the fundamental problem of child psychology. The elaboration of this problem has important theoretical significance since it is by determining the stages of mental development and by discovering the patterns of transition from one stage to the next that psychology eventually will solve the problem of the motive forces of mental development. We contend that every conception of the motive forces of mental development must first of all be tested on the "proving grounds" of theory of developmental stages.

The correct solution of the problem of developmental periods will in large measure determine the strategy employed in constructing a comprehensive educational system for the coming generation in our country. The practical significance of this problem will increase as we approach the point when we must elaborate the principles for a unified public system of education encompassing the entire period of childhood. We must emphasize the fact that the construction of such a system in compliance with the laws of developmental stages of childhood is possible only within a socialist society; for it is only in such a society that has a maximum interest in the full and harmonious development of the abilities of every one of its members and, consequently, in the fullest possible use of the potential of each developmental stage.

At the present time Soviet child psychology is guided by a conception of developmental stages based on the existing system of childhood education and upbringing. The processes of mental development are intimately connected with the child's education and upbringing; at the same time, the organization and structure of our educational system are themselves based on vast practical experience. It is natural that the division of childhood into stages for the aims and objectives of pedagogy approximates rather closely the real pattern. However, they do not coincide.

Most importantly, this breakdown can in no way provide a solution to the question of the motive forces in child's development, or to the patterns of transition from one stage to the next. The changes taking place in the course of education and upbringing reveal that the "pedagogical division of stages" lacks a sufficiently firm theoretical foundation and is unable to answer a number of essential practical questions; for example, when school education should begin, what special features education should exhibit at the time of a transition to a new stage, and so forth). Thus the existing concept of developmental stages is approaching a crisis. During the 1930s the question of developmental stages received great deal of attention from P. P. Blonskiy and L. S. Vygotsky, who thereby laid the foundations for the development of child psychology in the Soviet Union. Unfortunately, we have done no fundamental work on this problem since that time.

P. Blonskiy pointed to the fact that the processes of mental development are subject to historical change; he specifically pointed out how new stages of childhood have emerged over the course of history. He wrote: Modern man, under social conditions favorable for his development, develops further and more rapidly than the human being of earlier historical epochs. Hence childhood is not an eternal, immutable phenomenon: it is different at each different stage of evolution in the animal world, and it is different also at each different stage of mankind's own historical development. The more favorable the economic and cultural conditions of development, the faster its pace. In a communist society children will develop faster and will of course be much more developed than today's children at the same age .

Blonskiy continues: At the same time, we see that even youth (that is, the continuation of growth after puberty) is by no means a universal human characteristic: In the case of nations or social groups living under unfavourable conditions, growth and development cease at puberty. Thus youth has not been an eternal phenomenon; rather, it constitutes a late acquisition of mankind—indeed, one appearing almost exclusively within the historical epoch .

Blonskiy was an opponent of purely evolutionary notions about the course of child development. He considered child development to be primarily a process of qualitative transformations accompanied by sudden breaks and leaps. He wrote that "these changes may occur in the form of sharp crises, or they may take place gradually, almost imperceptibly. Let us agree to call those times in a child's life that are distinguished from one another by larger or smaller crises "periods" and "stages," respectively. Further, let us designate those times in a child's life that only flow into one another as "phases."

In the last years of his life, L. S. Vygotsky was in the process of writing a major work on child psychology. Although some chapters did achieve finished form, others have been preserved only as outlines or notes on reading material, Vygotsky himself prepared for publication the chapter entitled "The Problem of Age," which presents certain general implications and a theoretical analysis of the then existing materials—both Soviet and foreign—on the problem of stages of child mental development.

Vygotsky wrote: We may provisionally define psychological age as a specific epoch, cycle, or stage of development, as a definite, relatively self-contained period of development whose significance is determined by its place in the general developmental cycle and within each of which the general laws of development are expressed in a qualitatively distinct fashion.

In this sense we might compare age-levels in child development with the historical ages or eras in the development of mankind, with the evolutionary epochs in the development of organic life, or with geological epochs in the history of the earth's development. In the transition from one age-level to another we find the emergence of new structures that were absent in earlier periods; we can see a reorganization and alteration of the very course of development. Thus the development of the child is but a continuous transition from one age-level to another, accompanied by developmental changes in the child's personality. The study of child development is the study of the child's transition from one age-level to another and the change in his personality within each age-period as these changes occur under concrete socio-historical conditions .

"We already know," Vygotsky continues, "where the material foundations of a theory of age periods in childhood are to be sought. Only internal changes in the course of development itself, only sharp breaks and turning points during development, can give us a reliable foundation for determining those basic epochs in the formation of the child's personality that we call 'ages' ".

Vygotsky concludes his description of the basic features of transitional periods in development as follows: "Thus we see unveiled before us a perfectly regular and distinct pattern, full of the most profound meaning. Ages of stability are interrupted by ages of crisis . And these latter are the breaks and turning points in development, again confirming the thesis that the development of the child is a dialectical process, a process in which the transition from one stage to the next occurs not through evolution, but through revolution. Even if ages of crisis had not been discovered empirically, a theoretical analysis alone would have necessitated the inclusion of this concept in any scheme of development. As it is, theory is left only with the task of acknowledging and interpreting what has already been established through empirical investigation."

It is our view that Blonskiy's and Vygotsky's approaches to the problem of developmental stages must be maintained, but should be further developed in the light of present day knowledge concerning the mental development of the child. This would entail the following: first, a historical approach to the rate of development and to the question of the emergence of distinct stages of childhood in the course of the historical development of mankind; second, an approach to each age stage from the point of view of the position it occupies in the general cycle of the child's mental development; third, a concept of mental development as a dialectically contradictory process, a process that proceeds not along an evolutionary path, but along a path marked by breaks in continuity and the emergence of qualitatively new structures in the course of development; fourth, the discrimination of critical points in mental development as necessary and requisite turning points and the recognition of these critical points as important objective criteria of the transitions from one period to the next; and fifth, the discrimination of qualitatively different stages and, in connection with that, distinguishing among "periods," "stages," and "phases" in mental development.

Blonskiy and Vygotskiy were never able to put their

principles of developmental stages to work, owing to the absence of conditions for solving the problem of the motive forces of children's mental development. In the 1930s the answer to that problem revolved around developmental factors, around the question of the relative roles of environment and heredity in mental development.

Although both investigators tried to find a way out of the impasse created by the theory of "developmental factors," although they saw its methodological and practical scientific shortcomings, and although Vygotsky laid the groundwork for the elaboration of the problem of learning and development, none of their theoretical research led to a solution to the problem. This, in turn, impeded any special study of the problem of developmental stages.

One of the important achievements of Soviet psychology in the late 1930s was its introduction of the concept of activity into research on the genesis and development of the mind and consciousness . The result was a also in the principles for distinguishing its individual stages. And for the first time the solution to the problem of motive forces of children's mental development was found to have direct relevance to the question of the principles for distinguishing the specific stages in mental development.

This new notion was most clearly developed in the works of A. N. Leont'ev, who wrote: "Thus, in studying the mental development of the child we must proceed from the development of his activity as that activity arises from the given, concrete conditions of the child's life. . . . Life or activity in general is not built up mechanically from the particular forms of activity. At a given stage some types of activity will be more prominent, and more significant for the further development of the personality;

others, less so. Some types will play a leading role in development; others will play a minor role. That is why we should speak of the dependence of mental development not on activity in general, but on the dominant form of activity . In accordance with this we might say that each stage of mental development is characterized by one dominant relationship of the child to his environment, by one dominant activity within that given stage. The indication of a transition from one stage to another is precisely a shift in the dominant type of activity, the dominant relationship of the child to his surroundings."

The experimental investigations of A. N. Leont'ev, A. V. Zaporozhets, and their co-workers and the work of A. A. Smirnov, P. I. Zinchenko, and the followers of S. L. Rubinshteyn have demonstrated the dependence of the functional level of mental processes upon the nature of their involvement in this or that activity. In other words, mental processes are dependent on the motives and tasks of the activity in which they are involved; they are determined by the place they occupy in the structure of the activity . These facts have played an important role in the solution of a number of methodological problems in psychology.

Unfortunately, however, these new positions have not led to the elaboration of a corresponding theory of psychological development and developmental stages. In our opinion, the failure to develop such a theory is due to the fact that investigations of the psychological content of activity have neglected the objective-contextual aspect of activity, treating it as an aspect lying outside psychology. Attention has been devoted exclusively to the structure of activity, to the correlation of motives and tasks, actions and operations within activity. The solution to the problem of stages in mental development has also been restricted by the fact that we have studied only two types of activity directly related to mental development in childhood—play and learning. In fact, however, we can never understand the process of mental development without thoroughly investigating the objective-contextual aspect of activity, that is, without elucidating the question: With what particular aspects of reality does the child interact in performing this or that activity?

Up until the present time our concepts of the mental development of the child have suffered principally from a radical separation of processes of intellectual development from those of personality development. One result of this separation is that personality development, bereft of firm foundations, becomes reduced to the development of the need-affective or the need-motivational sphere.

As early as the 1930's Vygotsky pointed to the necessity of viewing the development of affect and intellect as a dynamic unity. But since that time the development of a child's cognitive powers and the development of the need-affective sphere have been regarded as completely independent, though parallel, processes. In pedagogical theory and practice this notion is reflected in the dichotomy between education, on the one hand, and upbringing, on the other.

Perhaps the clearest concept of an intellectual development divorced from the development of the need-affective sphere is that contained in the theory of J. Piaget. It is Piaget who has offered the most complete concept of how each individual stage in cognitive development emerges directly from the preceding stage . The principal shortcoming of this view lies in its inability to explain the transitions from one stage of intellectual development to the next. Why does the child proceed from the pre-operational stage to the concrete operational stage and then to the formal operational stage (Piaget's terms)? Why does the child advance from complex type thought to pre-conceptual thought, and finally to conceptual thought (Vygotsky's terms)? Why is there a transition from the stage of practical activity to the stage of images and then to the verbal-discursive stages (to use current terminology)? There is no clear-cut answer to these questions. And in the absence of such an answer the easiest way out is to allude either to "maturation" or to some other forces outside the actual process of mental development.

The development of the need-affective sphere—a development that, as we have already pointed out, is often identified with the development of personality—is viewed in an analogous fashion: its stages are arranged linearly, independent of cognitive development. Here, too, the result is that we are left with no explanation for the transition from one set of needs and motives for activity to another set.

Thus a peculiar dualism is read into mental development, which is then seen to follow two basic and parallel lines: the line of development of the need-motivational sphere and the line of development of the intellectual (cognitive) processes. It is this dualism and parallelism that we must overcome in order to understand the mental development of the child as a unitary process.

Underlying this dualism and parallelism is a naturalistic approach to the child's mental development, an approach that is characteristic of most foreign theories and one that, unfortunately, has not, yet been entirely eliminated from Soviet child psychology. Such an approach, first of all, views the child as an isolated individual for whom society is merely "an environing habitat" sui generis. Second, mental development is viewed merely as the process of adaptation to the conditions of life in society. Third, society is seen as the union of two mutually disjoint elements, a "world of things' and a "world of people," both of which are primordial elements of the given in this "environing habitat." Fourth, it is the development of two fundamentally distinct sets of adaptive mechanisms—for adaptation to the "world of things" and to the "world of people"—that constitutes mental development.

Mental development, then, is viewed as the development of adaptive mechanisms within two mutually disjoint systems: the system of "child -things" and the system of "child—other people." It is precisely this view that has given rise to the notion of two independent lines of mental development. These, in turn, are the source of two theories: Piaget's theory of the intellect and cognitive development, and the theory of the need-affective sphere and its development as expounded by Sigmund Freud and the neo-Freudians.

Despite differences in concrete psychological content, these conceptions are closely related in their basic interpretations of mental development as the development of adaptive mechanisms of behavior. For Piaget, the intellect is an adaptive mechanism, and its development is the development of forms of the child's adaptation to the "world of things." For Freud and the neo-Freudians, the mechanisms of substitution, censorship, displacement, etc., are mechanisms for the child's adaptation to the "world of people."

We should emphasize the fact that in viewing the adaptation of the child within the system of "child—things," the latter appear principally as physical objects with their spatial and physical properties. In viewing the adaptation of the child within the system of "child—other people," the latter appear as random individuals with their individual character traits, temperaments, etc. If things are viewed as physical objects and other people as random individuals, then the child's adaptation to these "two worlds" actually does seem to proceed along two parallel, fundamentally independent lines.

Overcoming this approach is not an easy matter, primarily because, for the child, the surrounding reality appears in two forms. We encountered this division of the child's reality into a "world of things" and a "world of people" in our experimental investigations of the nature of role-playing in preschool-age children. In attempting to elucidate the question of the sensitivity of role playing to these two spheres of reality, we in some cases acquainted children with things, their properties and their purposes. For example, during a trip to the zoo, we would acquaint the children with the animals, their habitat, external appearance, and so forth. Although toy animals were placed in the children's nursery after the trip, role-playing did not develop.

In other cases we would use such a trip to acquaint the children with the people who served on the zoo's staff, with their function stand interrelationships—with the cashier and the ticket-collector, with the guides, with the attendants who feed the animals, with the "wild animal doctor," and so on. After such a trip there was, as a rule, extended and interesting role-playing in which the children "modeled" the tasks of the adult's activity and the relations among the adults. Moreover, in these games the children's previously acquired knowledge about wild animals was given a context and meaning.

The results of that investigation testified to the fact that role-playing is sensitive primarily to the "world of people"—it is in their play that children "model" the purposes and motives of human activity and the norms of human relations. In addition, the investigation showed that for the child the surrounding world actually does appear divided into two spheres and that there is a close link between the child's activities in both (although in this investigation we were unable to shed light on the specific features of that link).

Overcoming the naturalistic concept of mental development calls for a radically new approach to the interrelation between child and society. We have been led to this conclusion by a special investigation of the historical emergence of role-playing. In contrast to the view that role playing is an eternal extra-historical phenomenon, we hypothesized that role playing emerged at a specific stage of social development, as the child's position in society changed in the course of history. Role-playing is an activity that is social in origin and, consequently, social in content.

This hypothesis concerning the historical origin of play is supported by a wealth of anthropological and ethnological material. This material demonstrates that role-playing emerges as the status of the child in society changed. The child's position in society has changed over the course of history, but at all times and places the child has been a part of society. In the early stages of mankind's development the link between the child and society was direct and immediate—from their very earliest years children lived a life in common with adults. The development of the child within this common life was a unified and integral process. The child constituted an organic part of the combined productive forces of the society, and his participation in it was limited only by his physical capacities.

As the means of production and as social relations grew more complex, the link between the child and society changed: this link, previously direct, now became mediated by education and the norms of upbringing. The system of "child—society," however, did not change, did not become a system of "child and society" (the conjunction "and" can, of course, imply contrast as well as combination). It would be more correct to speak of a system of the 'child in society." In the process of social development the functions of education and upbringing came in increasing measure to be taken over by the family, which itself became an independent economic unit. At the same time, the ties between the family and society became more and more indirect. The set of relations characterizing the "child in society" thereby became obscured and concealed by the system of relations "child—family," and within that, by the relationships between "the child and the individual adult."

If we look at the formation of personality in the system "child in society," we can see how the links in the systems " child- thing" and "child—individual adult" assume a radically different character. They change from two independent systems into one unified system. And, as a result, the content of each system is essentially changed. When we examine the system "child—thing" we now see that things, possessing definite physical and spatial, properties, appear to the child as social objects: it is the socially evolved modes of action with these objects that predominate.

The system "child—thing" is in reality the system "child—social object." Socially evolved modes of action with these objects are not given immediately as physical properties of the objects. We do not find inscribed on the object where and how it originated, how we may operate with it, how we can reproduce it. Therefore, that object cannot be mastered through adaptation, through a mere "accommodation" to its physical properties. This must take place internally; the child must go through a special process of learning the social modes of action with objects. In this process the physical properties of an object serve merely as referents for the child's orientation in his actions with that object.

As the child learns the socially evolved modes of action with objects, he is being shaped into a member of society, by a process that includes his intellectual, cognitive, and social forces. For the child himself (as well as for adults directly involved in the organized process of education and upbringing), this development appears primarily as the expansion of his sphere of assimilation of activity with objects expands outward to include more actions, and upward to a higher level of proficiency. It is in terms of these criteria that the child compares his own level and his own capabilities with those of adults and other children. In such a comparison the adult appears to the child not only as the bearer of social modes of action with objects but also as a person performing specific social tasks.

The distinctive features of the child's discovery of the human meaning of object actions have been shown in a number of investigations. For example, F. I. Fradkina has described how, at a certain stage in the acquisition of object actions, the small child begins to compare his own actions with those of the adult. This is demonstrated by the child's calling himself simultaneously by two names, his own name and the name of an adult; For example, imitating the action of an adult reading a newspaper or writing, a boy might say "Misha—Daddy," or a little girl, dressing her doll for bed, might refer to "Vera—Mommy." L. S. Slavina has shown in her investigations how the child, once he has discovered the human meaning of object actions, clings tenaciously to it, imparting that meaning to even the simplest manipulations.

These investigations were conducted on limited material concerning the development of object actions in very young children. But they do suggest that the child's acquisition of modes of action with objects lead him naturally to the adult as the bearer of the social aims of activity. It must be left to further investigation to determine the psychological mechanism of that transition in each concrete case and at each concrete stage of development.

The system "child—adult," in turn, also takes on a substantially different content. The adult no longer appears primarily as a collection of random and individual attributes, but as the bearer of certain types of social activity , as the performer of certain tasks, as one who exists in various relations to other people, and as a person who himself conforms to certain norms. But the ends and motives of an adult's activity are not outwardly visible from the activity itself.

Outwardly, the child sees that activity as the transformation and production of objects. The ends and motives of an activity are revealed only as that activity is carried out to its finished, real form within the totality of social relations; but the child unable to see the activity in that context.. Hence the need arises for a special process of learning the objectives and motives of human activity and the norms of human relations to which people conform as they act.

Unfortunately, the particular psychological features of that (learning) process have been inadequately investigated. Nevertheless, on the basis of what we know, we can offer the following hypothesis: the child learns the objectives, motives, and norms of the relations in adult activity by reproducing or imitating relations in his own activity, within the associations, and collectives to which he himself belongs. It is noting that in the learning process the child finds it necessary to learn new object actions that are required for performing adult activity. Thus the child sees the adult as the bearer of new and ever more complex modes of action with objects, of socially elaborated standards and norms that are necessary for orientation to the surrounding world.

Hence the child's activity within the systems "child—social object" and "child—social adult" represents a unitary process within which his personality is formed. In the course of historical development, however, this essentially unitary process of the child's life in society splits and develops two aspects. This split creates the preconditions for hypertrophied development of either of the two sides. The school in a class society exploits this possibility by rearing certain children primarily as performers of the operational and technical aspects of labor while educating others chiefly as bearers of the objectives and motives of that activity. It is only a class-structured society that is characterized by such exploitations of the historically evolved split in the unitary process of the child's life and development in society.

The theoretical ideas we have developed above are directly related to the problem of stages in the mental development of the child. Let us turn to the factual material accumulated in child psychology. From a multitude of investigations conducted in the last 20-30 years, we shall select those that have enriched our knowledge of the basic types of children's activity. Let us examine briefly the most important of these.

1. Until quite recently there was a great deal of uncertainty concerning the objective-contextual characteristics of infant activity. In particular, we were unclear as to which activity was dominant during this age. Some investigators (L. 1. Bozhovich and others) regarded the infant's need for external stimuli as primary. Consequently, the most important aspect of the child's activity was the development of orientative actions. Others, (Piaget and others) paid more attention to the development of sensomotor and manipulative activity. A third group emphasized the significance of the infants contact with adults.

In recent years, research conducted by M. I. Lisina and her associates has convincingly demonstrated that infants have a special form of activity for personal contact, activity that is directly emotional in nature. The animation that appears during the third month of the infant's life and that formally was considered a simple reaction to the adult (the strongest and most complex stimulus) is in reality a complex activity serving to produce contact with the adult and employing its own special means.

It is important to note the fact that this action appears long before the child begins to manipulate objects or before the act of grasping has been perfect . After grasping and manipulatory activity performed together with an adults has been achieved, communicative acts of contact are not absorbed into the broader framework of joint activity; they do not merge in the course of practical interactions with adults, but retain their own specific content and means. These and other investigations have shown that a deficit of emotional contact (and in all likelihood, a surfeit of such contact) exerts a decisive influence on mental development in this period.

Thus, we can assume that direct emotional contact with the adult represents the dominant activity of the infant; it is against the background of this activity and within this activity that orienting, sensorimotor, and manipulative actions take form.

These same investigators established the child's transition—at the end of infancy—to object activity proper , ie., to the acquisition of socially evolved modes of action involving objects. The learning of these actions is, of course, impossible without the participation of adults who demonstrate them to the child and perform them with him. The adult is merely one element—albeit a chief element—within the situation of object activity. Immediate emotional contact with the adult recedes to a subordinate role; the dominant role is now taken over by strictly practical cooperation in the activity at hand. The child is absorbed in the object and his manipulations of it. A number of researchers have repeatedly called attention to how the child seems thus to be bound up within a field of his direct actions. It is at this point that we observe the emergence of "object fetishism": the child seems not to notice the adult, who is "hidden" by the object and its properties.

Many investigators, both Soviet and foreign, have shown than an intensive process of learning object and instrumental operations takes place during this period, when so called "practical intelligence" is formed. Moreover, detailed investigations of the genesis of intelligence in the child, conducted by Piaget and his associates, have shown that it is precisely during this period that sensorimotor development takes place, a development that prepares for the emergence of the symbolic functions.

We have already referred to the studies of F. I. Fradkina, which showed how, in the process of learning an action, the action seems to become detached from the object on which it was originally learned: the action is transferred to other objects that, although similar, are not identical to the original object. In this fashion, actions are generalized. F. I. Fradkina showed that it is precisely through the detachment of actions from objects and their generalization that it becomes possible for the child to compare his actions with that of the adult; in this way the child begins to gain access to the meaning and aims of human activity.

These findings indicate that the dominant activity in early childhood is precisely object-instrumental activity, in their course of which the child learns socially evolved modes of action with objects.

At first glance this appears to be contradicted by the fact that it is during this period that the child develops verbal forms of communication with adults. From a being without speech whose contact with adults is through emotions and mimicry, the child turns into a speaking being who employs a grammar and a relatively broad vocabulary. However, analysis of the child's verbal communication reveals that he uses speech primarily as a means of furthering cooperation with adults within the context of their joint object activity.

In other words, it serves as a means of purely practical contact between child and adult. And what is more, we have reason to believe that object actions themselves, and the dexterity with which we perform them, are for the child a way of further cooperation with adults. These relations themselves are mediated by the child's object actions. Therefore, the intensive development of speech—if speech is seen as a means of a aiding cooperation with adults—does not contradict our contention that the dominant activity during this period is object activity, within which the child learns socially evolved modes of action with objects.

The work of Vygotsky, Leont'ev, and others has firmly established for Soviet psychology the fact that the dominant preschool activity is play in its most expanded form (role-playing). The significance of play in the mental development of the child at this age has many aspects. Its primary significance lies in the fact that in play the child imitates human actions in many ways , e.g., he assumes the role of the adult, the adult's functions and work in society; he reproduces object actions by generalizing them in representational thought; transfers meaning from one object to another, etc.

An object action, taken in isolation, does not have "written on it" the answers to questions such as: Why was it performed? What is its social meaning? Its actual motive? It is only when an object action becomes incorporated into a system of human relations that we can discover its true social meaning, its purposefulness as regards other people. This sort of "incorporation" also takes place in play.

Role-playing is an activity within which the child becomes oriented toward the most universal, the most fundamental, meanings of human activity. On this basis the child begins to strive for socially meaningful and socially valuable activity, and in so doing demonstrates the key factor in readiness for school. This is the chief significance of play for mental development; it is its dominant function.

In the early 1930s Vygotsky postulated that school instruction is the dominant element in the mental development of school-age children. Of course, not just any sort of instruction exerts such an influence on development: it is only "good instruction" that has such an effect. In ever increasing measure the quality of instruction is beginning to be judged by exactly how it influences the child's intellectual development. Psychologists have conducted a large number of experiments designed to determine how school instruction influences mental development. The limits of the present article do not permit us to examine all the different views. We will merely draw attention to the fact that a majority of investigators—however they may conceive of the inner mechanism of that influence and whatever significance they may ascribe to the various aspects of instruction (content, method, organization)—agree that instruction is the dominant factor in the intellectual development of the child in early school age.

The activity of formal learning, i.e., that activity through which the child acquires new knowledge and for which a system of instruction should provide proper guidance, is the dominant activity in this period. The intellectual and cognitive forces of the child are actively molded during the course of this process. The primacy of formal learning is also reflected in the fact that is this activity that mediates the whole system of the child's relations with surrounding adults.

Distinguishing the dominant activity during adolescence presents greater difficulties. These difficulties are associated with the fact that, for the adolescent, the primary activity is still school studies. For adults, success or failure in school continues to serve as the principal criterion for evaluating adolescents. Moreover, under present educational condition the transition to adolescence is not accompanied by any substantial outward changes. Yet it is precisely the transition to the adolescent period that psychology has distinguished as the most critical.

In the absence of any changes in the general conditions of life and activity, it is natural that psychologists have sought the cause of the transition to adolescence in the changes in the organism itself, in the process of sexual maturation that occurs in this period. Sexual development does, of course, exert an influence on personality development during this period, but it is not the primary influence. Like other changes connected with the intellectual and physical growth of the child, puberty exerts its influence indirectly, through the child's relations with the surrounding world, and through his comparing himself with adults and other adolescence, i.e., only within the whole complex of changes that occur at this time.

A number of investigations have shown how, in the

beginning of this period, a new sphere of life emerges. H. Wallon expressed this idea most clearly when he wrote: "When friendship and rivalry no longer are based on community or antagonism or tasks that are being, or remain to be, fulfilled ; when friendship and rivalry seek to express a spiritual affinity or difference; when it seems that they have personal aspects and are not linked to practical cooperation or conflict—this indicates the arrival of sexual maturity."

In recent years investigations conducted under D. B. El'konin and T. V. Dragunova have shown that a special activity emerges and develops in adolescence, an activity that consists in the establishment of intimate personal relations between adolescence. This activity has been termed the activity of social contact. It differs from other interrelations that occur in practical cooperation between peers in that its principle content concerns another adolescent as a human being with definite personal qualities.

In all forms of collected activity among adolescence we can observe how relations are subordinated to the "code of friendship." Interpersonal relations can be, and are, built on the basis not only of mutual respect but also of complete trust and a mutually shared private, inner world. This sphere of life shared in common among friends is particularly important in adolescence. The formation of the adolescent personality is greatly influenced by the formation of relations within the peer group, on the basis of the code of friendship. The code of friendship reproduces in its objective content the most universal norms of interrelations that hold for adults in society.

Social contact, then, is the specific form in which adult relationships are reproduced among adolescence, and the means by which adolescence becomes more thoroughly versed in the norms that guide adult society.

Thus it is reasonable to assume that the dominant activity during this period is social contact, the activity of building relations with friends on the basis of definite moral and ethical norms that mediate the actions of adolescence.

We can, however, go farther. Social contact, built on complete trust and a private world shared in common, is the activity in which the child's most universal views of life are formed, his views on human relations, on his own future—in short, the personal meanings of life. Thus we begin the formation of self-reflective awareness on the part of the child, his self consciousness as "social consciousness diverted inward". This, in turn, permits the emergence of new motives and objectives that direct the child's own activity toward the future and along the channels of education and career.

We have been able only to survey briefly the most important facts concerning the objective-contextual characteristics of the dominant types of activity that have been thus far distinguished, on the basis of which we might separate all the types into two large groups.

The first group includes activities that are accompanied by an intensive orientation in the fundamental meanings of human activity and by the learning of the objectives, motives, and norms of human relations, i.e., activities within a system of "child-social adult." There are of course essential differences between the direct emotional contact of the infant, role playing in young children, and the intimate personal contact between adolescence—differences both in terms of concrete content and in terms of the depth of the child's penetration into the sphere of motives and objectives of adult activity.

It is in fact these differences that allow us to picture the progression of different stages as a special sort of ladder for the progressive assimilation by the child of the sphere of motives and objectives in activity. Nevertheless, these activities do have a common basic content: it is precisely this group of activities that the primary development of the need-motivational sphere takes place.

The second group consists of activities, by means of which the child acquires both socially evolved modes of action with objects and the standards that distinguish the various aspects of those objects, i.e., these are activities in the system "child-social object." Of course, these are essential differences among the elements of this group. The very young child's manipulation of objects bears little resemblance to the learning activity of the young schoolchild, and even less resemblance to the vocational and career-oriented activity of older adolescence.

Indeed, what does mastering objective operations involving a spoon or glass have in common with mastering mathematics or grammar? Still they have one common feature: they are all elements of human culture. They have a common origin and a common place in the life of society; they all represent the result of a product of history. Through his learning of the socially evolved modes of action with objects, the child becomes more fully oriented within the objective world; his intellectual powers are shaped; he becomes a part of society's productive forces.

Here we should underscore one point: when we speak of the dominant activity and its significance for the child's development in this or that period, this is by no means meant to imply that the child might not be simultaneously developing in other directions as well. In each period, a child's life is many sided, and the activities of which his life is composed are varied. New sorts of activity appear; the child forms new relations with his surroundings. When a new activity becomes dominant, it does not cancel all previously existing activities: it merely alters their status within the overall system of relations between the child and his surroundings, which thereby becomes increasingly richer.

A sizable body of material in Soviet and foreign psychology permits us to discriminate two sharp transitions in children's mental development. First, the transition from early childhood to preschool age, usually termed the three-year-old crisis, and, second, the transition from early school age to adolescence, commonly referred to as the puberty crisis. A comparison of the symptoms of these two transitions reveals a great similarity between them. In both periods the child manifests a tendency toward independence as well as a series of negative phenomena connected with his relations with adults. Inserting these critical transitions into the scheme of developmental periods in childhood we arrive at the general pattern of periods, stages, and phases shown in the figure opposite.

As is evident, each period consists of two regularly connected stages. The first of these is the stage dominated by the learning of the learning of objectives, motives, and norms of human activity and by the development of the need-motivational sphere. At this point preparation is made for the transition to the second stage , dominated by the acquisition of modes of action with objects and the development of operational and technical abilities.

All three periods (early childhood, childhood, adolescent) are structured along the same lines and are composed of two regularly connected stages. The transition from one period to the next is marked by a discrepancy between the child's operational and technical capacities and the tasks and motives that constitute the fabric of which these capacities are woven.

We know very little about the transition from one

stage to the next or from one phase to the next. What, exactly, is the theoretical and practical significance of our hypotheses concerning the developmental stages and periodic scheme we have constructed on the basis of this hypotheses? First of all, the principle theoretical significance of our hypotheses lies in the fact that it permits us to overcome the dichotomy in child psychology between the development of the need-motivational aspect and the intellectual and cognitive aspect of the personality; it permits us to show their dialectical unity in opposition.

Second, our hypotheses enables us to view the process, of mental development as an ascending spiral rather than linearly. Third, it opens the way for studying the links between individual stages, for explaining how each "sets the stage" functionally for the following one. Fourth, our hypothesis breaks down development into periods and stages in a way that corresponds to the inner laws of that development, not to mere external factors.

The practical significance of the hypothesis consists in the fact that it serves as an aid in resolving the question of the susceptibility of the various stages of child development to particular types of influence; it offers a new approach to the problem of the links between the various institutions in our present educational system. According to the requirements flowing from this hypothesis, at the place where we have a break in our present system (preschool institutions-school) we should have a tighter organic link. And, conversely, where we now have continuity (primary grades-intermediate grade) there should actually be an abrupt changeover to a new educational system.

5

Teacher-student Relationship

A careful analysis of the teacher-student relationship at any level inside or outside the school, reveals its fundamentally *narrative* character This relationship involves a narrating Subject (the teacher) and patient, listening objects (the students). The contents, whether values or empirical dimensions of reality, tend in the process of being narrated to become lifeless and petrified. Education is suffering from narration sickness.

The teacher talks about reality as if it were motionless, static, compartmentalised, and predictable. Or else he expounds on a topic completely alien to the existential experience of the students. His task is to "fill" the students with the contents of his narration — contents which are detached from reality, disconnected from the totality that engendered them and could give them significance. Words are emptied of their concreteness and become a hollow, alienated, and alienating verbosity.

The outstanding characteristic of this narrative education, then, is the sonority of words, not their transforming power. "Four times four is sixteen; the capital of Para is Belem." The student records, memorizes, and repeats these phrases without perceiving what four times four really means, or realizing the true significance of "capital" in the affirmation "the capital of

Para is Belem," that is, what Belem means for Para and what Para means for Brazil.

Narration (with the teacher as narrator) leads the students to memorize mechanically the narrated content. Worse yet, it turns them into "containers," into "receptacles" to be "filled" by the teacher. The more completely she fills the receptacles, the better a teacher she is. The more meekly the receptacles permit themselves to be filled, the better students they are.

Education thus becomes an act of depositing, in which the students are the depositories and the teacher is the depositor. Instead of communicating, the teacher issues communiques and makes deposits which the students patiently receive, memorize, and repeat. This is the "banking" concept of education, in which the scope of action allowed to the students extends only as far as receiving, filing, and storing the deposits. They do, it is true, have the opportunity to become collectors or cataloguers of the things they store. But in the last analysis, it is the people themselves who are filed away through the lack of creativity, transformation, and knowledge in this (at best) misguided system. For apart from inquiry apart from the praxis, individuals cannot be truly human. Knowledge emerges only through invention and re-invention, through the restless, impatient, continuing, hopeful inquiry, human beings pursue in the world, with the world, and with each other.

In the banking concept of education, knowledge is a gift bestowed by those who consider themselves knowledgeable upon those whom they consider to know nothing. Projecting an absolute ignorance onto others, a characteristic of the ideology of oppression, negates education and knowledge as processes of inquiry. The teacher presents himself to his students as their necessary opposite; by considering their ignorance absolute, he justifies his own existence. The students, alienated like the slave in the Hegelian dialectic, accept their ignorance as justifying the teacher's existence — but, unlike the slave, they never discover that they educate the teacher.

The *raison d'etre* of libertarian education, on the other hand, lies in its drive towards reconciliation. Education must begin with the solution of the teacher-student contradiction, by reconciling the poles of the contradiction so that both are simultaneously teachers *and* students.

This solution is not (nor can it be) found in the banking concept. On the contrary, banking education maintains and even stimulates the contradiction through the following attitudes and practices, which mirror oppressive society as a whole:

— the teacher teaches and the students are taught;

— the teacher knows everything and the students know nothing;

— the teacher thinks and the students are thought about;

— the teacher talks and the students listen — meekly;

— the teacher disciplines and the students are disciplined;

— the teacher chooses and enforces his choice, and the students comply;

— the teacher acts and the students have the illusion of acting through the action of the teacher;

— the teacher chooses the program content, and the students (who were not consulted) adapt to it;

— the teacher confuses the authority of knowledge with his or her own professional authority, which she and he sets in opposition to the freedom of the students;

— the teacher is the Subject of the learning process, while the pupils are mere objects.

It is not surprising that the banking concept of education regards men as adaptable, manageable beings. The more students work at storing the deposits entrusted to them, the less they develop the critical consciousness which would result from their intervention in the world as transformers of that world. The more completely they accept the passive role imposed on them, the more they tend simply to adapt to the world as it is and to the fragmented view of reality deposited in them.

The capability of banking education to minimize or annul the students' creative power and to stimulate their credulity serves the interests of the oppressors, who care neither to have the world revealed nor to see it transformed. The oppressors use their "humanitarianism" to preserve a profitable situation. Thus they react almost instinctively against any experiment in education which stimulates the critical faculties and is not content with a partial view of reality but always seeks out the ties which link one point to another and one problem to another.

Indeed, the interests of the oppressors lie in "changing the consciousness of the oppressed, not the situation which oppresses them"; for the more the oppressed can be led to adapt to that situation, the more easily they can be dominated. To achieve this end, the oppressors use the banking concept of education in conjunction with a paternalistic social action apparatus, within which the oppressed receive the euphemistic title of "welfare recipients." They are treated as individual cases, as marginal persons who deviate from the general configuration of a "good, organized, and just" society. The oppressed are regarded as the pathology of the healthy society, which must therefore adjust these "incompetent and lazy" folk to its own patterns by changing their mentality. These marginals need to be "integrated," "incorporated" into the healthy society that they have "forsaken."

The truth is, however, that the oppressed are not "marginals," are not people living "outside" society. They have always been "inside" — inside the structure which made them "beings for others." The solution is not to "integrate" them into the structure of oppression, but to transform that structure so that they can become "beings for themselves." Such transformation, of course, would undermine the oppressors' purposes; hence their utilization of the banking concept of education to avoid the threat of student *conscientizacao.*

The banking approach to adult education, for example, will never propose to students that they critically consider reality. It will deal instead with such vital questions as whether Roger gave green grass to the goat, and insist upon the importance of learning that on the contrary, Roger gave green grass to the rabbit. The "humanism" of the banking approach masks the effort to turn women and men into automatons — the very negation of their ontological vocation to be more fully human.

Those who use the banking approach, knowingly or unknowingly (for there are innumerable well-intentioned bank-clerk teachers who do not realize that they are serving only to dehumanize), fail to perceive that the deposits themselves contain contradictions about reality. But, sooner or later, these contradictions may lead formerly passive students to turn against their domestication and the attempt to domesticate reality. They may discover through existential experience that their present way of life is irreconcilable with their vocation to become fully human. They may perceive through their relations with reality that reality is really a *process*, undergoing constant transformation. If men and women are searchers and their ontological vocation is humanization, sooner or later they may perceive the contradiction in which banking education seeks to maintain them, and then engage themselves in the struggle for their liberation.

But the humanist, revolutionary educator cannot wait for this possibility to materialize. From the outset, her efforts must coincide with those of the students to engage in critical thinking and the quest for mutual humanization. His efforts must be imbued with a profound trust in people and their creative power. To achieve this, they must be partners of the students in their relations with them.

The banking concept does not admit to such partnership — and necessarily so. To resolve the teacher-student contradiction, to exchange the role of depositor, prescriber, domesticator, for the role of student among students would be to undermine the power of oppression and serve the cause of liberation.

Implicit in the banking concept is the assumption of a dichotomy between human beings and the world: a person is merely *in* the world, not *with* the world or with others; the individual is spectator, not re-creator. In this view, the person is not a conscious being (*corpo consciente*); he or she is rather the possessor of a consciousness: an empty "mind" passively open to the reception of deposits of reality from the world outside.

It follows logically from the banking notion of consciousness that the educator's role is to regulate the way the world "enters into" the students. The teacher's task is to organize a process which already occurs spontaneously to "fill" the students by making deposits of information which he or she considers to constitute true knowledge. And since people "receive" the world as passive entities, education should make them more passive still, and adapt them to the world. The educated individual is the adapted person, because she or he is a better "fit" for the world. Translated into practice, this concept is well suited to the purposes of the oppressors, whose tranquility rests on how well people fit the world the oppressors have created, and how little they question it.

The more completely the majority adapt to the purposes which the dominant minority prescribe for them (thereby depriving them of the right to their own purposes), the more easily the minority can continue to prescribe. The theory and practice of banking education serve this end quite efficiently. Verbalistic lessons, reading requirements, the methods for evaluating knowledge, the distance between the teacher and the taught, the criteria for promotion: everything in this ready-to-wear approach serves to obviate thinking.

The bank-clerk educator does not realize that there is no true security in his hypertrophied role, that one must seek to live *with* others in solidarity. One cannot impose oneself, nor even merely co-exist with one's students. Solidarity requires true communication, and the concept by which such an educator is guided fears and proscribes communication.

Yet only through communication can human life hold meaning. The teacher's thinking is authenticated only by the authenticity of the students' thinking. The teacher cannot think for her students, nor can she impose her thought on them. Authentic thinking, thinking that is concerned about *reality*, does not take place in ivory tower isolation, but only in communication. If it is true that thought has meaning only when generated by action upon the world, the subordination of students to teachers becomes impossible.

Because banking education begins with a false understanding of men and women as objects, it cannot promote the development of what From calls "biophily," but instead produces its opposite: "necrophily."

> While life is characterized by growth in a structured, functional manner, the necrophilous person loves all that does not grow, all that is mechanical. The necrophilous person is driven by the desire to transform the organic into the inorganic, to approach life mechanically, as if all living persons were things. ... Memory, rather than experience; having, rather than being, is what counts. The necrophilous person can relate to an object — a flower or a person — only if he possesses it; hence a threat to his possession is a threat to himself; if he loses possession he loses contact with the world. ... He loves control, and in the act of controlling he kills life.

Oppression — overwhelming control — is necrophilic; it is nourished by love of death, not life. The banking concept of education, which serves the interests of oppression, is also necrophilic. Based on a mechanistic, static, naturalistic, spatialized view of consciousness, it transforms students into receiving objects. It attempts to control thinking and action, leads women and men to adjust to the world, and inhibits their creative power.

When their efforts to act responsibly are frustrated, when they find themselves unable to use their faculties, people suffer. "This suffering due to impotence is rooted in the very fact that the human equilibrium has been disturbed"_But the inability to act which causes people's anguish also causes them to reject their impotence, by attempting ... to restore [their] capacity to act. But can [they], and how? One way is to submit to and identify with a person or group having power By this symbolic participation in another person's life, [men have] the illusion of acting, when in reality [they] only submit to and become a part of those who act.

Populist manifestations perhaps best exemplify this type of behaviour by the oppressed, who, by identifying with charismatic leaders, come to feel that they themselves are active and effective. The rebellion they express as they emerge in the historical process is motivated by that desire to act effectively. The dominant elites consider the remedy to be more domination and repression, carried out in the name of freedom, order, and social peace (that is, the peace of the elites). Thus they can condemn — logically from their point of view — "the violence of a strike by workers and [can] call upon the state in the same breath to use violence in putting down the strike."

Education as the exercise of domination stimulates the credulity of students, with the ideological intent (often not perceived by educators) of indoctrinating them to adapt to the world of oppression. This accusation is not made in the naive hope that the dominant elites will thereby simply abandon the practice. Its objective is to call the attention of true humanists to the fact that they cannot use banking educational methods in the pursuit of liberation, for they would only negate that very pursuit. Nor may a revolutionary society inherit these methods from an oppressor society. The revolutionary society which practices banking education is either misguided or mistrusting of people. In either event it is threatened by the specter of reaction.

Unfortunately, those who espouse the cause of liberation are themselves surrounded and influenced by the climate which generates the banking concept, and often do not perceive its true significance or its dehumanizing power. Paradoxically, then, they utilize this same instrument of alienation in what they consider an effort to liberate. Indeed, some "revolutionaries" brand as "innocents," "dreamers," or even "reactionaries" those who would challenge this educational practice. But one does not liberate people by alienating them. Authentic liberation — the process of humanization — is not another deposit to be made in men. Liberation is a praxis: the action and reflection of men and women upon their world in order to transform it. Those truly committed to the cause of liberation can accept neither the mechanistic concept of consciousness as an empty vessel to be filled, nor the use of banking methods of domination (propaganda, slogans — deposits) in the name of liberation.

Those truly committed to liberation must reject the banking concept in its entirety, adopting instead a concept of women and men as conscious beings, and consciousness as consciousness intent upon the world. They must abandon the educational goal of deposit-making and replace it with the posing of the problems of human beings in their relations with the world. "Problem-posing" education, responding to the essence of consciousness — intentionality — rejects communiques and embodies communication. It epitomizes the special characteristic of consciousness: being *conscious of* not only as intent on objects but as turned in upon itself in a Jasperian "split" — consciousness as consciousness *of* consciousness.

Liberating education consists in acts of cognition, not transferrals of information. It is a learning situation in which the cognizable object (far from being the end of the cognitive act) intermediates the cognitive actors — teacher on the one hand and students on the other. Accordingly the practice of problem-posing education entails at the outset that the teacher-student contradiction be resolved. Dialogical relations — indispensable to the capacity of cognitive actors to cooperate in perceiving the same cognizable object — are otherwise impossible.

Indeed, problem-posing education, which breaks with the vertical patterns characteristic of banking education, can fulfil its function as the practice of freedom only if it can overcome the above contradiction. Through dialogue, the teacher-of-the-students and the students-of-the-teacher cease to exist and a new term emerges: teacher-student with students-teachers.

The teacher is no longer merely the-one-who-teaches, but one who is himself taught in dialogue with the students, who in turn while being taught also teach. They become jointly responsible for a process in which all grow. In this process, arguments based on "authority" are no longer valid; in order to function, authority must be *on the side of* freedom, not against it. Here, no one teaches another, nor is anyone self-taught. People teach each other, mediated by the world, by the cognizable objects which in banking education are "owned" by the teacher.

The banking concept (with its tendency to dichotomize everything) distinguishes two stages in the action of the educator. During the first he cognizes a cognizable object while he prepares his lessons in his study or his laboratory; during the second, he expounds to his students about that object. The students are not called upon to know, but to memorize the contents narrated by the teacher. Nor do the students practice any act of cognition, since the object towards which that act should be directed is the property of the teacher rather than a medium evoking the critical reflection of both teacher and students. Hence in the name of the "preservation of culture and knowledge" we have a system which achieves neither true knowledge nor true culture.

The problem-posing method does not dichotomize the activity of the teacher-student: she is not "cognitive" at one point and "narrative" at another. She is always "cognitive," whether preparing a project or engaging in dialogue with the students. He does not regard cognizable objects as his private property but as the object of reflection by himself and the students. In this way the problem-posing educator constantly re-forms his reflections in the reflection of the students. The students — no longer docile listeners — are now critical co-investigators in dialogue with the teacher. The teacher presents the material to the students for their consideration, and re-considers her earlier considerations as the students express their own. The role of the problem-posing educator is to create, together with the students, the conditions under which knowledge at the level of the *doxa* is superseded by true knowledge, at the level of the *logos*.

Whereas banking education anesthetizes and inhibits creative power, problem-posing education involves a constant unveiling of reality. The former attempts to maintain the *submersion* of consciousness; the latter strives for the *emergence* of consciousness and *critical intervention* in reality.

Students, as they are increasingly posed with problems relating to themselves in the world and with the world, will feel increasingly challenged and obliged to respond to that challenge. Because they apprehend the challenge as interrelated to other problems within a total context, not as a theoretical question, the resulting comprehension tends to be increasingly critical and thus constantly less alienated. Their response to the challenge evokes new challenges, followed by new understandings; and gradually the students come to regard themselves as committed.

Education as the practice of freedom — as opposed to education as the practice of domination — denies that man is abstract, isolated, independent, and unattached to the world; it also denies that the world exists as a reality apart from people. Authentic reflection considers neither abstract man nor the world without people, but pea-pie in their relations with the world. In these relations consciousness and world are simultaneous: consciousness neither precedes the world nor follows it.

La conscience et le monde sont dormes d'un meme coup: exterieur par essence a la conscience, le monde est, par essence relatif a elle.

In one of our culture circles in Chile, the group was discussing the anthropological concept of culture. In the midst of the discussion, a peasant who by banking standards was completely ignorant said: "Now I see that without man there is no world." When the educator responded: "Let's say, for the sake of argument, that all the men on earth were to die, but that the earth itself remained, together with trees, birds, animals, rivers, seas, the stars. ... wouldn't all this be a world?" "Oh no," the peasant replied emphatically. "There would be no one to say: 'This is a world'."

As women and men, simultaneously reflecting on themselves and on the world, increase the scope of their perception, they begin to direct their observations towards previously inconspicuous phenomena:

In problem-posing education, people develop their power to perceive critically *the way they exist* in the world *with which* and *in which* they find themselves; they come to see the world not as a static reality but as a reality in process, in transformation. Although the dialectical relations of women and men with the world exist independently of how these relations are perceived (or whether or not they are perceived at all), it is also true that the form of action they adopt is to a large extent a function of how they perceive themselves in the world. Hence, the teacher-student and the students-teachers reflect simultaneously on themselves and the world without dichotomizing this reflection from action, and thus establish an authentic form of thought and action.

Once again, the two educational concepts and practices under analysis come into conflict. Banking education (for obvious reasons) attempts, by mythicizing reality, to conceal certain facts which explain the way human beings exist in the world; problem-posing education sets itself the task of demythologizing. Banking education resists dialogue; problem-posing education regards dialogue as indispensable to the act of cognition which unveils reality. Banking education treats students as objects of assistance; problem-posing education makes them critical thinkers.

Banking education inhibits creativity and domesticates (although it cannot completely destroy) the *intentionality* of consciousness by isolating consciousness from the world, thereby denying people their ontological and historical vocation of becoming more fully human. Problem-posing education bases itself on creativity and stimulates true reflection and action upon reality, thereby responding to the vocation of persons as beings who are authentic only when engaged in inquiry and creative transformation. In sum: banking theory and practice, as immobilizing and fixating forces, fail to acknowledge men and women as historical beings; problem-posing theory and practice take the people's historicity as their starting point.

Problem-posing education affirms men and women as beings in the process of *becoming* — as unfinished, uncompleted beings in and with a likewise unfinished reality. Indeed, in contrast to other animals who are unfinished, but not historical, people know themselves to be unfinished; they are aware of their incompletion. In this incompletion and this awareness lie the very roots of education as an exclusively human manifestation. The unfinished character of human beings and the transformational character of reality necessitate that education be an ongoing activity.

Education is thus constantly remade in the praxis. In order to *be,* it must *become.* Its "duration" (in the Bergsonian meaning of the word) is found in the interplay of the opposites *permanence* and *change.* The banking method emphasizes permanence and becomes reactionary; problem-posing education — which accepts neither a "well-behaved" present nor a predetermined fixture — roots itself in the dynamic present and becomes revolutionary.

Problem-posing education is revolutionary futurity. Hence it is prophetic (and, as such, hopeful). Hence, it corresponds to the historical nature of humankind. Hence, it affirms women and men as beings who transcend themselves, who move forward and look ahead, for whom immobility represents a fatal threat, for whom looking at the past must only be a means of understanding more clearly what and who they are so that they can more wisely build the fixture. Hence, it identifies with the movement which engages people as beings aware of their incompletion — an historical movement which has its point of departure, its Subjects and its objective.

The point of departure of the movement lies in the people themselves. But since people do not exist apart from the world, apart from reality the movement must begin with the human-world relationship. Accordingly, the point of departure must always be with men and women in the "here and now," which constitutes the situation within which they are submerged, from which they emerge, and in which they intervene. Only by starting from this situation — which determines their perception of it — can they begin to move. To do this authentically they must perceive their state not as fated and unalterable, but merely as limiting — and therefore challenging.

Whereas the banking method directly or indirectly reinforces men's fatalistic perception of their situation, the problem-posing method presents this very situation to them as a problem. As the situation becomes the object of their cognition, the naive or magical perception which produced their fatalism gives way to perception which is able to perceive itself even as it perceives reality, and can thus be critically objective about that reality.

A deepened consciousness of their situation leads people to apprehend that situation as an historical reality susceptible of transformation. Resignation gives way to the drive for transformation and inquiry, over which men feel themselves to be in control, if people, as historical beings necessarily engaged with other people in a movement of inquiry, did not control that movement, it would be (and is) a violation of their humanity. Any situation in which some individuals prevent others from engaging in the process of inquiry is one of violence. The means used are not important; to alienate human beings from their own decision-making is to change them into objects.

This movement of inquiry must be directed towards humanization — the people's historical vocation. The pursuit of full humanity however, cannot be carried out in isolation or individualism, but only in fellowship and solidarity; therefore it cannot unfold in the antagonistic relations between oppressors and oppressed. No one can be authentically human while he prevents others from being so. Attempting *to be more* human, individualistically, leads to *having more,* egotistically a form of dehumanization. Not that it is not fundamental *to have* in order *to be* human. Precisely because it *is* necessary, some men's *having* must not be allowed to constitute an obstacle to others *having,* must not consolidate the power of the former to crush the latter.

Problem-posing education, as a humanist and liberating praxis, posits as fundamental that the people subjected to domination must fight for their emancipation. To that end, it enables teachers and students to become Subjects of the educational process by overcoming authoritarianism and an alienating intellectualism; it also enables people to overcome their false perception of reality. The world — no longer something to be described with deceptive words — becomes the object of that transforming action by men and women which results in their humanization.

Problem-posing education does not and cannot serve the interests of the oppressor. No oppressive order could permit the oppressed to begin to question: Why? While only a revolutionary society can carry out this education in systematic terms, the revolutionary leaders need not take full power before they can employ the method. In the revolutionary process, the leaders cannot utilize the banking method as an interim measure, justified on grounds of expediency with the intention of *later* behaving in a genuinely revolutionary fashion. They must be revolutionary — that is to say dialogical — from the outset.

6

Authentic Education

An unauthentic word, one which is unable to transform reality, results when dichotomy is imposed upon its constitutive elements. When a word is deprived of its dimension of action, reflection automatically suffers as well; and the word is changed into idle chatter, into *verbalism*, into an alienated and alienating "blah." It becomes an empty word, one which cannot denounce the world, for denunciation is impossible without a commitment to transform, and there is no transformation without action.

On the other hand, if action is emphasized exclusively to the detriment of reflection, the word is converted into *activism*. The latter — action for action's sake — negates the true praxis and makes dialogue impossible. Either dichotomy, by creating unauthentic forms of existence, creates also unauthentic forms of thought which reinforce the original dichotomy.

Human existence cannot be silent nor can it be nourished by false words, but only by true words, with which men and women transform the world. To exist humanly is to *name* the world, to change it. Once named, the world in its turn reappears to the namers as a problem and requires of them a new *naming*. Human beings are not built in silence, but in word, in work, in action-reflection.

But while to say the true word — which is work, which is praxis — is to transform the world, saying that word is not the privilege of some few persons, but the right of everyone. Consequently no one can say a true word alone — nor can she say it *for* another, in a prescriptive act which robs others of their words.

Dialogue is the encounter between men, mediated by the world, in order to name the world. Hence, dialogue cannot occur between those who want to name the world and those who do not wish this naming — between those who deny others the right to speak their word and those whose right to speak has been denied them. Those who have been denied their primordial right to speak their word must first reclaim this right and prevent the continuation of this dehumanizing aggression.

If it is in speaking their word that people, by naming the world, transform it dialogue imposes itself as the way by which they achieve significance as human beings. Dialogue is thus an existential necessity. And since dialogue is the encounter in which the united reflection and action of the dialoguers are addressed to the world which is to be transformed and humanized, this dialogue cannot be reduced to the act of one person's "depositing" ideas in another; nor can it become a simple exchange of ideas to be "consumed" by the discussants. Nor yet is it a hostile, polemical argument between those who are committed neither to the naming of the world, nor to the search for truth, but rather to the imposition of their own truth.

Because dialogue is an encounter among women and men who name the world, it must not be a situation where some name on behalf of others. It is an act of creation; it must not serve as a crafty instrument for the domination of one person by another. The domination implicit in dialogue is that of the world by the dialoguers;

it is conquest of the world for the liberation of humankind.

Dialogue cannot exist, however, in the absence of a profound love for the world and for people. The naming of the world, which is an act of creation and re-creation, is not possible if it is not infused with love. Love is at the same time the foundation of dialogue and dialogue itself. It is thus necessarily the task of responsible Subjects and cannot exist in a relation of domination. Domination reveals the pathology of love: sadism in the dominator and masochism in the dominated. Because love is an act of courage, not of fear, love is commitment to others.

No matter where the oppressed are found, the act of love is commitment to their cause — the cause of liberation. And this commitment, because it is loving, is dialogical. As an act of bravery, love cannot be sentimental; as an act of freedom, it must not serve as a pretext for manipulation. It must generate other acts of freedom; otherwise, it is not love. Only by abolishing the situation of oppression is it possible to restore the love which that situation made impossible.

Dialogue further requires an intense faith in humankind, faith in their power to make and remake, to create and re-create, faith in their vocation to be more fully human (which is not the privilege of an elite, but the birthright of all). Faith in people is an *a priori* requirement for dialogue; the "dialogical man" believes in others even before he meets them face to face. His faith, however, is not naive. The "dialogical man" is critical and knows that although it is within the power of humans to create and transform, in a concrete situation of alienation individuals may be impaired in the use of that power. Far from destroying his faith in the people, however, this possibility strikes him as a challenge to which he must respond. He is convinced that the power to create and transform, even when thwarted in concrete situations, tends to be reborn. And that rebirth can occur — not gratuitously, but in and through the struggle for liberation — in the supersedence of slave labour by emancipated labour which gives zest to life. Without this faith in people, dialogue is a farce which inevitably degenerates into paternalistic manipulation.

Founding itself upon love, humility, and faith, dialogue becomes a horizontal relationship of which mutual trust between the dialoguers is the logical consequence. It would be a contradiction in terms if dialogue — loving, humble, and full of faith — did not produce this climate of mutual trust, which leads the dialoguers into ever closer partnership in the naming of the world. Conversely, such trust is obviously absent in the anti-dialogics of the banking method of education. Whereas faith in humankind is an *a priori* requirement for dialogue, trust is established by dialogue. Should it founder, it will be seen that the preconditions were lacking.

False love, false humility, and feeble faith in others cannot create trust. Trust is contingent on the evidence which one party provides the others of his true, concrete intentions; it cannot exist if that party's words do not coincide with their actions. To say one thing and do another — to take one's own word lightly — cannot inspire trust. To glorify democracy and to silence the people is a farce; to discourse on humanism and to negate people is a lie.

Nor yet can dialogue exist without hope. Hope is rooted in men's incompletion, from which they move out in constant search — a search which can be carried out only in communion with others. Hopelessness is a form of silence, of denying the world and fleeing from it. The dehumanization resulting from an unjust order is not a cause for despair but for hope, leading to the incessant pursuit of the humanity denied by injustice. Hope, however, does not consist in crossing one's arms and waiting.

Finally, true dialogue cannot exist unless the dialoguers engage in critical thinking — thinking which discerns an indivisible solidarity between the world and the people and admits of no dichotomy between them — thinking which perceives reality as process, as transformation, rather than as a static entity — thinking which does not separate itself from action, but constantly immerses itself in temporality without fear of the risks involved.

Critical thinking contrasts with naive thinking, which sees "historical time as a weight, a stratification of the acquisitions and experiences of the past," from which the present should emerge normalized and "well-behaved." For the naive thinker, the important thing is accommodation to this normalized "today." For the critic, the important thing is the continuing transformation of reality, in behalf of the continuing humanization of men. In the words of Pierre Furter:

> The goal will no longer be to eliminate the risks of temporality by clutching to guaranteed space, but rather to temporalize space... The universe is revealed to me not as space, imposing a massive presence to which I can but adapt, but as a scope, a domain which takes shape as I act upon it.

For naïve thinking, the goal is precisely to hold fast to this guaranteed space and adjust to it. By thus denying temporality, it denies itself as well.

Only dialogue, which requires critical thinking, is also capable of generating critical thinking. Without dialogue there is no communication, and without communication there can be no true education. Education which is able to resolve the contradiction between teacher and student takes place in a situation in which both address their act of cognition to the object by which they are mediated. Thus, the dialogical character of education as the practice of freedom does not begin when the teacher-student meets with the students-teachers in a pedagogical situation, but rather when the former first asks herself or himself *what* she or he will dialogue with the latter *about*. And preoccupation with the content of dialogue is really preoccupation with the program content of education.

For the anti-dialogical banking educator, the question of content simply concerns the program about which he will discourse to his students; and he answers his own question, by organizing his own program. For the dialogical, problem-posing teacher-student, the program content of education is neither a gift nor an imposition — bits of information to be deposited in the students — but rather the organized, systematized, and developed "representation" to individuals of the things about which they want to know more.

Authentic education is not carried on by "A" *for* "B" or by "A" *about* "B," but rather by "A" *with* "B," mediated by the world-a world which impresses and challenges both parties, giving rise to views or opinions about it. These views, impregnated with anxieties, doubts, hopes, or hopelessness, imply significant themes on the basis of which the program content of education can be built. In its desire to create an ideal model of the "good man," a naïvely conceived humanism often overlooks the concrete, existential, present situation of real people. Authentic humanism, in Pierre Furter's words, "consists in permitting the emergence of the awareness of our full humanity, as a condition and as an obligation, as a situation and as a project." We simply cannot go to the laborers — urban or peasant — in the banking style, to give them "knowledge" or to impose upon them the model of the "good man" contained in a program whose content we have ourselves organized. Many political and educational plans have failed because their authors designed them according to their own personal views of reality, never once taking into account (except as mere objects of their actions) the *men-in-a-situation* to whom their program was ostensibly directed.

For the truly humanist educator and the authentic revolutionary, the object of action is the reality to be transformed by them together with other people — not other men and women themselves. The oppressors are the ones who act upon the people to indoctrinate them and adjust them to a reality which must remain untouched.

Unfortunately, however, in their desire to obtain the support of the people for revolutionary action, revolutionary leaders often fall for the banking line of planning program content from the top down. They approach the peasant or urban masses with projects which may correspond to their own view of the world, but not to that of the people. They forget that their fundamental objective is to fight alongside the people for the recovery of the people's stolen humanity, not to "win the people over" to their side. Such a phrase does not belong in the vocabulary of revolutionary leaders, but in that of the oppressor The revolutionary's role is to liberate, and be liberated, with the people — not to win them over.

In their political activity, the dominant elites utilize the banking concept to encourage passivity in the oppressed, corresponding with the latter's "submerged" state of consciousness, and take advantage of that passivity to "fill" that consciousness with slogans which create even more fear of freedom. This practice is incompatible with a truly liberating course of action, which, by presenting the oppressor's slogans as a problem, helps the oppressed to "eject" those slogans from within themselves. After all the task of the humanists is surely not that of pitting their slogans against the slogans of the oppressors, with the oppressed as the testing ground, "housing" the slogans of first one group and then the other. On the contrary, the task of the humanists is to see that the oppressed become aware of the fact that as dual beings, "housing" the oppressors within themselves, they cannot be truly human.

This task implies that revolutionary leaders do not go to the people in order to bring them a message of "salvation," but in order to come to know through dialogue with them both their *objective situation* and their *awareness* of that situation — the various levels of perception of themselves and of the world in which and with which they exist. One cannot expect positive results from an educational or political action program which fails to respect the particular view of the world held by the people. Such a program constitutes cultural invasion, good intentions notwithstanding.

The starting point for organizing the program content of education or political action must be the present, existential, concrete situation, reflecting the aspirations of the people. Utilizing certain basic contradictions, we must pose this existential, concrete, present situation to the people as a problem which challenges them and requires a response — not just at the intellectual level, but at the level of action.

The present situation, must never provide the people with programs which have little or nothing to do with their own preoccupations, doubts, hopes, and fears — programs which at times in fact increase the fears of the oppressed consciousness. It is not our role to speak to the people about our own view of the world, nor to attempt to impose that view on them, but rather to dialogue with the people about their view and ours. The world, manifested variously in their action, reflects their *situation* in the world. Educational and political action which is not critically aware of this situation runs the risk either of "banking" or of preaching in the desert.

Often, educators and politicians speak and are not understood because their language is not attuned to the concrete situation of the people they address. Accordingly their talk is just alienated and alienating rhetoric. The language of the educator or the politician (and it seems more and more clear that the latter must also become an educator, in the broadest sense of the word), like the language of the people, cannot exist without thought; and neither language nor thought can exist without a structure to which they refer In order to communicate effectively educator and politician must understand the structural conditions in which the thought and Ianguage of the people are dialectically framed.

It is to the reality which mediates men, and to the perception of that reality held by educators and people. The investigation of what I have termed the people's "thematic universe"- the complex of their "generative themes" — inaugurates the dialogue of education as the practice of freedom. The methodology of that investigation must likewise be dialogical, affording the opportunity both to discover generative themes and to stimulate people's awareness in regard to these themes. Consistent with the liberating purpose of dialogical education, the object of the investigation is not persons (as if they were anatomical fragments), but rather the thought-language with which men and women refer to reality, the levels at which they perceive that reality, and their view of the world, in which their generative themes are found.

Before describing a "generative theme" more precisely, which will also clarify what is meant by a "minimum thematic universe," it seems to me indispensable to present a few preliminary reflections. The concept of a generative theme is neither an arbitrary invention nor a working hypothesis to be proved. If it were a hypothesis to be proved, the initial investigation would seek not to ascertain the nature of the theme, but rather the very existence or non-existence of themes themselves.

In that event, before attempting to understand the theme in its richness, its significance, its plurality, its transformations, and its historical composition, first have to verify whether or not it is an objective fact; only then could we proceed to apprehend it. Although an attitude of critical doubt is legitimate, it does appear possible to verify the reality of the generative theme — not only through one's own existential experience, but also through critical reflection on the human-world relationship and on the relationships between people implicit in the former.

This point deserves more attention. One may well remember — trite as it seems — that, of the uncompleted beings, man is the only one to treat not only his actions but his very self as the object of his reflection; this capacity distinguishes him from the animals, which are unable to separate themselves from their activity and thus are unable to reflect upon it. In this apparently superficial distinction lie the boundaries which delimit the action of each in his life space. Because the animals' activity is an extension of themselves, the results of that activity are also inseparable from themselves; animals can neither set objectives nor infuse their transformation of nature with any significance beyond itself. Moreover, the "decision" to perform this activity belongs not to them but to their species. Animals are, accordingly, fundamentally "beings in themselves."

Unable to decide for themselves, unable to objectify either themselves or their activity, lacking objectives which they themselves have set, living "submerged" in a world to which they can give no meaning, lacking a "tomorrow" and a "today" because they exist in an overwhelming present, animals are ahistorical. Their ahistorical life does not occur in the "world," taken in its strict meaning; for the animal, the world does not constitute a "not-I" which could set him apart as an "I."

The human world, which is historical, serves as a mere prop for the "being in itself." Animals are not challenged by the configuration which confronts them; they are merely stimulated. Their life is not one of risk-taking, for they are not aware of taking risks. Risks are not challenges perceived upon reflection, but merely "noted" by the signs which indicate them; they accordingly do not require decision-making responses.

Consequently, animals cannot commit themselves. Their ahistorical condition does not permit them to "take on" life. Because they do not "take it on," they cannot construct it; and if they do not construct it, they cannot transform its configuration. Nor can they know themselves to be destroyed by life, for they cannot expand their "prop" world into a meaningful, symbolic world which includes culture and history. As a result animals do not "animalize" their configuration in order to animalize themselves — nor do they "deanimalize" themselves. Even in the forest, they remain "beings-in-themselves," as animal-like there as in the zoo.

In contrast the people — aware of their activity and the world in which they are situated, acting in function of the objectives which they propose, having the seat of their decisions located in themselves and in their relations with the world and with others, infusing the world with their creative presence by means of the transformation they effect upon it — unlike animals, not only live but exist; and their existence is historical. Animals live out their lives on an atemporal, flat, uniform "prop"; humans exist in a world which they are constantly re-creating and transforming. For animals, "here" is only a habitat with which they enter into contact; for people, "here" signifies not merely a physical space, but also an historical space.

Strictly speaking, "here," "now" "there," "tomorrow;" and "yesterday" do not exist for the animal, whose life, lacking self-consciousness, is totally determined. Animals cannot surmount the limits imposed by the "here," the "now;" or the "there."

Humans, however, because they are aware of themselves and thus of the world — because they are *conscious beings* — exist in a dialectical relationship between the determination of limits and their own freedom. As they separate themselves from the world, which they objectify, as they separate themselves from their own activity, as they locate the seat of their decisions in themselves and in their relations with the world and others, people overcome the situations which limit them: the "limit-situations." Once perceived by individuals as fetters, as obstacles to their liberation, these situations stand out in relief from the background, revealing their true nature as concrete historical dimensions of a given reality. Men and women respond to the challenge with actions which Vieira Pinto calls "limit-acts": those directed at negating and overcoming, rather than passively accepting, the given.

Thus, it is not the limit-situations in and of themselves which create a climate of hopelessness, but rather how they are perceived by women and men at a given historical moment: whether they appear as fetters or as insurmountable barriers. As critical perception is embodied in action, a climate of hope and confidence develops which leads men to attempt to overcome the limit-situations. This objective can be achieved only through action upon the concrete, historical reality in which limit-situations historically are found. As reality is transformed and these situations are superseded, new ones will appear; which in turn will evoke new limit-acts.

The prop world of animals contains no limit-situations, due to its ahistorical character. Similarly, animals lack the ability to exercise limit-acts, which require a decisive attitude towards the world: separation from and objectification of the world in order to transform it. Organically bound to their prop, animals do not distinguish between themselves and the world.

Accordingly, animals are not limited by limit-situations — which are historical — but rather by the entire prop. And the appropriate role for animals is not to relate to their prop (in that event the prop would be a world), but to adapt to it. Thus, when animals "produce" a nest, a hive, or a burrow, they are not creating products which result from "limit-acts," that is, transforming responses. Their productive activity is subordinated to the satisfaction of a physical necessity which is simply stimulating, rather than challenging. "An animal's product belongs immediately to its physical body, whilst man freely confronts his product."

Only products which result from the activity of a being but do not belong to its physical body (though these products may bear its seal), can give a dimension of meaning to the context, which thus becomes a world. A being capable of such production (who thereby is necessarily aware of himself is a "being for himself" could no longer *be* if she or he were not *in the process of being* in the world with which he or she relates; just as the world would no longer exist if this being did not exist.

The difference between animals — who (because their activity does not constitute limit-acts) cannot create products detached from themselves — and humankind- who through their action upon the world create the realm of culture and history — is that only the latter are beings of the praxis. Only human beings *are* praxis — the praxis which, as the reflection and action which truly transform reality; is the source of knowledge and creation. Animal activity; which occurs without a praxis, is not creative; people's transforming activity is.

It is as transforming and creative beings that humans, in their permanent relations with reality, produce not only material goods — tangible objects — but also social institutions, ideas, and concepts. Through their continuing praxis, men and women simultaneously create history and become historical-social beings. Because — in contrast to animals — people can tri-dimensionalize time into the past, the present, and the future, their history, in function of their own creations, develops as a constant process of transformation within which epochal units materialize. These epochal units are not closed periods of time, static compartments within which people are confined. Were this the case, a fundamental condition of history — its continuity — would disappear. On the contrary, epochal units interrelate in the dynamics of historical continuity.

An epoch is characterized by a complex of ideas, concepts, hopes, doubts, values, and challenges in dialectical interaction with their opposites, striving towards plenitude. The concrete representation of many of these ideas, values, concepts, and hopes, as well as the obstacles which impede the people's full humanization, constitute the themes of that epoch. These themes imply others which are opposing or even antithetical; they also indicate tasks to be carried out and fulfilled. Thus, historical themes are never isolated, independent, disconnected, or static; they are always interacting dialectically with their opposites. Nor can these themes be found anywhere except in the human-world relationship. The complex of interacting themes of an epoch constitutes its "thematic universe."

Confronted by this "universe of themes" in dialectical contradiction, persons take equally contradictory positions: some work to maintain the structures, others to change them. As antagonism deepens between themes which are the expression of reality, there is a tendency for the themes and for reality itself to be mythicized, establishing a climate of irrationality and sectarianism. This climate threatens to drain the themes of their deeper significance and to deprive them of their characteristically dynamic aspect.

In such a situation, myth-creating irrationality itself becomes a fundamental theme. Its opposing theme, the critical and dynamic view of the world, strives to unveil reality, unmask its mythicization, and achieve a full realization of the human task: the permanent transformation of reality in favour of the liberation of people.

In the last analysis, the *themes* both contain and are contained in *limit-situations;* the *tasks* they imply require *limit-acts*. When the themes are concealed by the limit-situations and thus are not clearly perceived, the corresponding tasks — people's responses in the form of historical action — can be neither authentically nor critically fulfilled. In this situation, humans are unable to transcend the limit — situations to discover that beyond these situations — and in contradiction to them — lies an *untested feasibility*.

In sum, limit-situations imply the existence of persons who are directly or indirectly served by these situations, and of those who are negated and curbed by them. Once the latter come to perceive these situations as the frontier between being and being more human, rather than the frontier between being and nothingness, they begin to direct their increasingly critical actions towards achieving the untested feasibility implicit in that perception.

On the other hand, those who are served by the present limit-situation regard the untested feasibility as a threatening limit-situation which must not be allowed to materialize, and act to maintain the status quo. Consequently, liberating actions upon an historical milieu must correspond not only to the generative themes but to the way in which these themes are perceived. This requirement in turn implies another: the investigation of meaningful thematics.

Generative themes can be located in concentric circles, moving from the general to the particular. The broadest epochal unit, which includes a diversified range of units and sub-units — continental, regional, national, and so forth — contains themes of a universal character. The fundamental theme of our epoch to be that of domination — which implies its opposite, the theme of *liberation*, as the objective to be achieved. It is this tormenting theme which gives our epoch the anthropological character mentioned earlier. In order to achieve humanization, which presupposes the elimination of dehumanizing oppression, it is absolutely necessary to surmount the limit-situations in which people are reduced to things.

Within the smaller circles, limit-situations characteristic of societies (on the same continent or on different continents) which through these themes and limit-situations share historical similarities. For example, underdevelopment, which cannot be understood apart from the relationship of dependency, represents a limit-situation characteristic of societies of the Third World. The task implied by this limit-situation is to overcome the contradictory relation of these "object"-societies to the metropolitan societies; this task constitutes the untested feasibility for the Third World.

Any given society within the broader epochal unit contains; in addition to the universal, continental, or historically similar themes, its own particular themes, its own limit-situations. Within yet smaller circles, thematic diversifications can be found within the same society, divided into areas and sub-areas, all of which are related to the societal whole. These constitute epochal sub-units. For example, within the same national unit one can find the contradiction of the "coexistence of the non-contemporaneous."

Within these sub-units, national themes may or may not be perceived in their true significance. They may simply be *felt* — sometimes not even that. But the nonexistence of themes within the sub-units is absolutely impossible. The fact that individuals in a certain area do not perceive a generative theme, or perceive it in a distorted way, may only reveal a limit-situation of oppression in which people are still submerged.

In general, a dominated consciousness which has not yet perceived a limit-situation in its totality apprehends only its epiphenomena and transfers to the latter the inhibiting force which is the property of the limit-situation. This fact is of great importance for the investigation of generative themes. When people lack a critical understanding of their reality; apprehending it in fragments which they do not perceive as interacting constituent elements of the whole, they cannot truly know that reality. To truly know it, they would have to reverse their starting point: they would need to have a total vision of the context in order subsequently to separate and isolate its constituent elements and by means of this analysis achieve a clearer perception of the whole.

Equally appropriate for the methodology of thematic investigation and for problem-posing education is this effort to present significant dimensions of an individual's contextual reality; the analysis of which will make it possible for him to recognize the interaction of the various components. Meanwhile, the significant dimensions, which in their turn are constituted of parts in interaction, should be perceived as dimensions of total reality. In this way a critical analysis of a significant existential dimension makes possible a new, critical attitude towards the limit-situations.

The perception and comprehension of reality are rectified and acquire new depth. When carried out with a methodology of *conscientizacao* the investigation of the generative theme contained in the minimum thematic universe (the generative themes in interaction) thus introduces or begins to introduce women and men to a critical form of thinking about their world.

In the event, however, that human beings perceive reality as dense, impenetrable, and enveloping, it is indispensable to proceed with the investigation by means of abstraction. This method does not involve reducing the concrete to the abstract (which would signify the negation of its dialectical nature), but rather maintaining both elements as opposites which interrelate dialectically in the act of reflection. This dialectical movement of thought is exemplified perfectly in the analysis of a concrete existential, "coded" situation. Its "decoding" requires moving from the abstract to the concrete; this requires moving from the part to the whole and then returning to the parts; this in turn requires that the Subject recognize himself in the object (the coded concrete existential situation) and recognize the object as a situation in which he finds himself, together with other Subjects. If the decoding is *well* done, this movement of flux and reflux from the abstract to the concrete which occurs in the analysis of a coded situation leads to the supersedence of the abstraction *by* the critical perception of the concrete, which has already ceased to be a dense, impenetrable reality.

When an individual is presented with a coded existential situation (a sketch or photograph which leads by abstraction to the concreteness of existential reality), his tendency is to "split" that coded situation. In the process of decoding, and facilitates the discovery of the interaction among the parts of the disjoined whole. This whole (the coded situation), which previously had been only diffusely apprehended, begins to acquire meaning as thought flows back to it from the various dimensions.

Since, however, the coding is the representation of an existential situation, the decoder tends to take the step from the representation to the very concrete situation in which and with which she finds herself. It is thus possible to explain conceptually why individuals begin to behave differently with regard to objective reality, once that reality has ceased to look like a blind alley and has taken on its true aspect: a challenge which human beings must meet.

In all the stages of decoding, people exteriorize their view of the world. And in the way they think about and face the world — fatalistically, dynamically, or statically — their generative themes may be found. A group which does not concretely express a generative thematics — a fact which might appear to imply the nonexistence of themes — is, on the contrary, suggesting a very dramatic theme: *the theme of silence.* The theme of silence suggests a structure of mutism in face of the overwhelming force of the limit-situations.

The generative theme cannot be found in people, divorced from reality; nor yet in reality, divorced from people; much less in "no man's land." It can only be apprehended in the human-world relationship. To investigate the generative theme is to investigate people's thinking about reality and people's action upon reality, which is their praxis. For precisely this reason, the methodology proposed requires that the investigators and the people (who would normally be considered objects of that investigation) should act as *co-investigators.* The more active an-attitude men and women take in regard to the exploration of their thematics, the more they deepen their critical awareness of reality and, in spelling out those thematics, take possession of that reality.

Some may think it inadvisable to include the people as investigators in the search for their own meaningful thematics: that their intrusive influence (n. b., the "intrusion" of those who are most interested — or ought to be — in their own education) will "adulterate" the findings and thereby sacrifice the objectivity of the investigation. This view mistakenly presupposes that themes exist in their original objective purity outside people-as if themes were *things.* Actually, themes exist in people in their relations with the world, with reference to concrete facts. The same objective fact could evoke different complexes of generative themes in different epochal sub-units. There is, therefore, a relation between the given objective fact the perception women and men have of this fact and the generative themes.

A meaningful thematics is expressed by people, and a given moment of expression will differ from an earlier moment, if they have changed their perception of the objective facts to which the themes refer. From the investigator's point of view, the important thing is to detect the starting point at which the people visualize the "given" and to verify whether or not during the process of investigation any transformation has occurred in their way of perceiving reality. (Objective reality, of course, remains unchanged. If the perception of that reality changes in the course of the investigation, that fact does not impair the validity of the investigation.)

The aspirations, the motives, and the objectives implicit in the meaningful thematics are *human* aspirations, motives, and objectives. They do not exist "out there" somewhere, as static entities; *they are occurring*. They are as historical as human beings themselves; consequently, they cannot be apprehended apart from them. To apprehend these themes and to understand them is to understand both the people who embody them and the reality to which they refer. But — precisely because it is not possible to understand these themes apart from people — it is necessary that those concerned understand them as well. Thematic investigation thus becomes a common striving towards awareness of reality and towards self-awareness, which makes this investigation a starting point for the educational process or for cultural action of a liberating character.

The real danger of the investigation is not that the supposed objects of the investigation, discovering themselves to be co-investigators, might "adulterate" the analytical results. On the contrary the danger lies in the risk of shifting the focus of the investigation from the meaningful themes to the people themselves, thereby treating the people as objects of the investigation. Since this investigation is to serve as a basis for developing an educational program in which teacher-student and students-teachers combine their cognitions of the same object, the investigation itself must likewise be based on reciprocity of action.

Thematic investigation, which occurs in the realm of the human, cannot be reduced to a mechanical act. As a process of search, of knowledge, and thus of creation, it requires the investigators to discover the interpenetration of problems, in the linking of meaningful themes. The investigation will be most educational when it is most critical, and most critical when it avoids the narrow outlines of partial or "focalized" views of reality, and sticks to the comprehension of *total* reality. Thus, the process of searching for the meaningful thematics should include a concern for the links between themes, a concern to pose these themes as problems, and a concern for their historical-cultural context.

Just as the educator may not elaborate a program to present *to* the people, neither may the investigator elaborate "itineraries" for researching the thematic universe, starting from points which he has predetermined. Both education and the investigation designed to support it must be "sympathetic" activities, in the etymological sense of the won That is, they must consist of communication and of the common experience of a reality perceived in the complexity of its constant "becoming."

The investigator who, in the name of scientific objectivity, transforms the organic into something inorganic, what is becoming into what is, life into death, is a person who fears change. He or she sees in change (which is not denied, but neither is it desired) not a sign of life, but a sign of death and decay. He or she does want to study change-but in order to stop it not in order to stimulate or deepen it. However, in seeing change as a sign of death and in making people the passive objects of investigation in order to arrive at rigid models, one betrays their own character as a killer of life.

The investigation of thematics involves the investigation of the people's thinking-thinking which occurs only in and among people together seeking out reality. Even if the people's thinking is superstitious or naïve, it is only as they rethink their assumptions in action that they can change. Producing and acting upon their own ideas — not consuming those of others — must constitute that process.

People, as beings "in a situation," find themselves rooted in temporal-spatial conditions which mark them and which they also mark. They will tend to reflect on their own "situationality" to the extent that they are challenged by it to act upon it. Human beings *are* because they *are in* a situation. And they *will be more* the more they not only critically reflect upon their existence but critically act upon it.

Reflection upon situationality is reflection about the very condition of existence: critical thinking by means of which people discover each other to be "in a situation." Only as this situation ceases to present itself as a dense, enveloping reality or a tormenting blind alley, and they can come to perceive it as an objective-problematic situation — only then can commitment exist. Humankind *emerge* from their *submersion* and acquire the ability to *intervene* in reality as it is unveiled. *Intervention* in reality — historical awareness itself — thus represents a step forward from *emergence,* and results from the *conscientizacao* of the situation. *Conscientizacao* is the deepening of the attitude of awareness characteristic of all emergence.

Every thematic investigation which deepens historical awareness is thus really educational, while all authentic education investigates thinking. The more educators and the people investigate the people's thinking, and are thus jointly educated, the more they continue to investigate. Education and thematic investigation, in the problem-posing concept of education, are simply different moments of the same process.

In contrast with the antidialogical and non-communicative "deposits" of the banking method of education, the program content of the problem-posing method — dialogical par excellence — is constituted and organized by the students' view of the world, where their own generative themes are found. The content thus constantly expands and renews itself. The task of the dialogical teacher in an interdisciplinary team working on the thematic universe revealed by their investigation is to "re-present" that universe to the people from whom she or he first received it-and "re-present" it not as a lecture, but as a problem.

Let us say, for example, that a group has the responsibility of coordinating a plan for adult education in a peasant area with a high percentage of illiteracy. The plan includes a literacy campaign and a post-literacy phase. During the former stage, problem-posing education seeks out and investigates the "generative word"; in the post-literacy stage, it seeks out and investigates the "generative theme."

Let us here, however; consider only the investigation of the generative themes or the meaningful thematics. Once the investigators have determined the area in which they will work and have acquired a preliminary acquaintance with the area through secondary sources, they initiate the first stage of the investigation. This beginning (like any beginning in any human activity) involves difficulties and risks which are to a certain point normal, although they are not always evident in the first contact with the individuals of the area. In this first contact the investigators need to get a significant number of persons to agree to an informal meeting during which they can talk about the objectives of their presence in the area. In this meeting they explain the reason for the investigation, how it is to be carried out, and to what use it will be put; they further explain that the investigation will be impossible without a relation of mutual understanding and trust.

If the participants agree both to the investigation and to the subsequent process, the investigators should call for volunteers among the participants to serve as assistants. These volunteers will gather a series of necessary data about the life of the area. Of even greater importance, however, is the active presence of these volunteers in the investigation.

Meanwhile, the investigators begin their own visits to the area, never forcing themselves, but acting as sympathetic observers with an attitude of *understanding* towards what they see. While it is normal for investigators to come to the area with values which influence their perceptions, this does not mean that they may transform the thematic investigation into a means of imposing these values. The only dimension of these values which it is hoped the people whose thematics are being investigated will come to share (it is presumed that the investigators possess this quality) is a critical perception of the world, which implies a correct method of approaching reality in order to unveil it. And critical perception cannot be imposed. Thus, from the very beginning, thematic investigation is expressed as an educational pursuit as cultural action.

During their visits, the investigators set their critical "aim" on the area under study, as if it were for them an enormous, unique, living "code" to be deciphered. They regard the area as a totality and visit upon visit attempt to "split" it by analyzing the partial dimensions which impress them. Through this process they expand their understanding of how the various parts interact which will later help them penetrate the totality itself.

During this decoding stage, the investigators observe certain moments of the life of the area — sometimes directly, sometimes by means of informal conversations with the inhabitants. They register everything in their notebooks, including apparently unimportant items: the way the people talk, their style of life, their behavior at church and at work. They record the idiom of the people: their expressions, their vocabulary and their syntax (not their incorrect pronunciation, but rather the way they construct their thought).

It is essential that the investigators observe the area under varying circumstances: labor in the fields, meetings of a local association (noting the behavior of the participants, the language used, and the relations between the officers and the members), the role played by women and by young people, leisure hours, games and sports, conversations with people in their homes (noting examples of husband-wife and parent-child relationships). No activity must escape the attention of the investigators during the initial survey of the area.

After each observation visit, the investigator should draw up a brief report to be discussed by the entire team, m order to evaluate the preliminary findings of both the professional investigators and the local assistants. To facilitate the participation of the assistants, the evaluation meetings should be held in the area itself.

The evaluation meetings represent a second stage in the decoding of the unique living code. As each person, in his decoding essay, relates how he perceived or felt a certain occurrence or situation, his exposition challenges all the other decoders by re-presenting to them the same reality upon which they have themselves been intent. At this moment they "re-consider" through the "considerations" of others, their own previous "consideration." Thus the analysis of reality made by each individual decoder sends them all back, dialogically to the disjoined whole which once more becomes a totality evoking a new analysis by the investigators, following which a new evaluative and critical meeting will be held. Representatives of the inhabitants participate in all activities as members of the investigating team.

The more the group divide and reintegrate the whole, the more closely they approach the nuclei of the principal and secondary contradictions which involve the inhabitants of the area. By locating these nuclei of contradictions, the investigators might even at this stage be able to organize the program content of their educational action. Indeed, if the content reflected these contradictions, it would undoubtedly contain the meaningful thematics of the area. And one can safely affirm that action based on these observations would be much more likely to succeed than that based on "decisions from the top."

The investigators should not, however, be tempted by this possibility The basic thing, starting from the initial perception of these nuclei of contradictions (which include the principal contradiction of society as a larger epochal unit) is to study the inhabitants' level of awareness of these contradictions.

Intrinsically, these contradictions constitute limit-situations, involve themes, and indicate tasks. If individuals are caught up in and are unable to separate themselves from these limit-situations, their theme in reference to these situations is *fatalism*, and the task implied by the theme is *the lack of a task.* Thus, although the limit-situations are objective realities which call forth needs in individuals, one must investigate with these individuals their level of awareness of these situations.

A limit-situation as a concrete reality can call forth from persons in different areas (and even in sub-areas of the same area) quite opposite themes and tasks. Thus, the basic concern of the investigators should be to concentrate on the knowledge of what Goldman calls "real consciousness" and the "potential consciousness.

Real consciousness [is] the result of the multiple obstacles and deviations that the different factors of empirical reality put into opposition and submit for realization by [the] potential consciousness.

Real consciousness implies the impossibility of perceiving the "untested feasibility" which lies beyond the limit-situations. But whereas the untested feasibility cannot be achieved at the level of "real [or present] consciousness," it can be realized through "testing action" which reveals its hitherto unperceived viability. The untested feasibility and real consciousness are related, as are testing action and potential consciousness. Goldman's concept of "potential consciousness" is similar to what Nicolaï terms "unperceived practicable solutions" (our "untested feasibility"), in contrast to "perceived practicable solutions" and "presently practiced solutions," which correspond to Goldman's "real consciousness." Accordingly, the fact that the investigators may in the first stage of the investigation approximately apprehend the complex of contradictions does not authorize them to begin to structure the program content of educational action. This perception of reality is still their own, not that of the people.

It is with the apprehension of the complex of contradictions that the second stage of the investigation begins. Always acting as a team, the investigators will select some of these contradictions to develop the codifications to be used in the thematic investigation. Since the codifications (sketches or photographs) are the *objects* which mediate the decoders in their critical analysis, the preparation of these codifications must be guided by certain principles other than the usual ones for making visual aids.

The first requirement is that these codifications must necessarily represent situations familiar to the individuals whose thematics are being examined, so that they can easily recognize the situations (and thus their own relation to them). It is inadmissible (whether during the process of investigation or in the following stage, when the meaningful thematics are presented as program content) to present pictures of reality unfamiliar to the participants.

The latter procedure (although dialectical, because individuals analyzing an unfamiliar reality could compare it with their own and discover the limitations of each) cannot precede the more basic one dictated by the participants' state of submersion, that is, the process in which individuals analyzing their own reality become aware of their prior, distorted perceptions and thereby come to have a new perception of that reality.

An equally fundamental requirement for the preparation of the codifications is that their thematic nucleus be neither overly explicit nor overly enigmatic. The former may degenerate into mere propaganda, with no real decoding to be done beyond stating the obviously predetermined content. The latter runs the risk of appearing to be a puzzle or a guessing game. Since they represent existential situations, the codifications should be simple in their complexity and offer various decoding possibilities in order to avoid the brain-washing tendencies of propaganda. Codifications are not slogans;

they are cognizable objects, challenges towards which the critical reflection of the decoders should be directed.

In order to offer various possibilities of analysis in the decoding process, the codifications should be organized as a "thematic fan." As the decoders reflect on the codifications, the codifications should open up in the direction of other themes. This opening up (which does not occur if the thematic content is either too explicit or too enigmatic) is indispensable to the perception of the dialectical relations which exist between the themes and their opposites. Accordingly the codifications reflecting an existential situation must objectively constitute a totality. Its elements must interact in the makeup of the whole.

In the process of decoding, the participants externalize their thematics and thereby make explicit their "real consciousness" of the world. As they do this, they begin to see how they themselves acted while actually experiencing the situation they are now analyzing, and thus reach a "perception of their previous perception." By achieving this awareness, they come to perceive reality differently; by broadening the horizon of their perception, they discover more easily in their "background awareness" the dialectical relations between the two dimensions of reality.

By stimulating "perception of the previous perception" and "knowledge of the previous knowledge," decoding stimulates the appearance of a new perception and the development of new knowledge. The new perception and knowledge are systematically continued with the inauguration of the educational plan, which transforms the untested feasibility into testing action, as potential consciousness supersedes real consciousness.

Preparing the codifications further requires that insofar as possible they should represent contradictions "inclusive" of others which constitute the system of contradictions of the area under study. As each of these "inclusive" codifications is prepared, the other contradictions "contained" therein should also be codified. The decoding of the former will be dialectically clarified by the decoding of the latter

In this connection, a very valuable contribution to our method has been made by Gabriel Bode, a young Chilean civil servant in one of the most significant Chilean governmental institutions: the *Instituto deDesarrollo Agropecuario* (INDAP). During his use of this method in the post-literacy stage, Bode observed that the peasants became interested in the discussion only when the codification related directly to their felt needs. Any deviation in the codification, as well as any attempt by the educator to guide the decoding discussion into other areas, produced silence and indifference.

On the other hand, he observed that even when the codification centered on their felt needs the peasants could not manage to concentrate systematically on the discussion, which often digressed to the point of never reaching a synthesis. Also, they almost never perceived the relationship of their felt needs to the direct and indirect causes of these needs. One might say that they failed to perceive the untested feasibility lying beyond the limit-situations which engendered their needs.

Bode then decided to experiment with the simultaneous projection of different situations; in this technique lies the value of his contribution. Initially, he projects a very simple codification of an existential situation. He terms his first codification "essential"; it represents the basic nucleus and opens up into a thematic fan extending to "auxiliary" codifications. After the essential codification is decoded, the educator maintains its projected image as a reference for the participants and successively projects alongside it the auxiliary codifications. By means of the latter, which are directly related to the essential codification, he sustains the vivid interest of the participants, who are thereby enabled to reach a synthesis.

The great achievement of Gabriel Bode is that, by means of the dialectics between the essential and the auxiliary codifications, he has managed to communicate to the participants a sense of *totality*. Individuals who were *submerged* in reality, merely *feeling* their needs, *emerge* from reality and perceive the *causes* of their needs. In this way, they can go beyond the level of real consciousness to that of potential consciousness much more rapidly.

Once the codifications have been prepared and all their possible thematic facets have been studied by the interdisciplinary team, the investigators begin the third stage of the investigation by returning to the area to initiate decoding dialogues in the "thematic investigation circles." These discussions, which decode the material prepared in the preceding stage, are taped for subsequent analysis by the interdisciplinary team. In addition to the investigator acting as decoding co-ordinator, two other specialists — a psychologist and a sociologist — attend the meetings. Their task is to note and record the significant (and apparently insignificant) reactions of the decoders.

During the decoding process, the co-ordinator must not only listen to the individuals but must challenge them, posing as problems both the codified existential situation and their own answers. Due to the cathartic force of the methodology, the participants of the thematic investigation circles externalize a series of sentiments and opinions about themselves, the world, and others, that perhaps they would not express under different circumstances.

In one of the thematic investigations carried out in Santiago, a group of tenement residents discussed a scene showing a drunken man walking on the street and three young men conversing on the corner; The group participants commented that "the only one there who is productive and useful to his country is the souse who is returning home after working all day for low wages and who is worried about his family because he can't take care of their needs. He is the only worker He is a decent worker and a souse like us."

The investigator had intended to study aspects of alcoholism. He probably would not have elicited the above responses if he had presented the participants with a questionnaire he had elaborated himself. If asked directly, they might even have denied ever taking a drink themselves. But in their comments on the codification of an existential situation they could recognize, and in which they could recognize themselves, they said what they really felt.

There are two important aspects to these declarations. On the one hand, they verbalize the connection between earning low wages, feeling exploited, and getting drunk — getting drunk as a flight from reality, as an attempt to overcome the frustration of inaction, as an ultimately self-destructive solution. On the other hand, they manifest the need to rate the drunkard highly. He is the "only one useful to his country, because he works, while the others only gab." After praising the drunkard, the participants then identify themselves with him, as workers who also drink — "decent workers."

In contrast, imagine the failure of a moralistic educator, sermonizing against alcoholism and presenting as an example of virtue something which for these men is not a manifestation of virtue. In this and in other cases, the only sound procedure is the *conscientizacao* of the situation, which should be attempted from the start of the thematic investigation. (Obviously, *conscientizacao* does not stop at the level of mere subjective perception of a situation, but through action prepares men for the struggle against the obstacles to their humanization.)

In another experience, this time with peasants, the unchanging motif during an entire discussion of a situation depicting work in the fields was the demand for an increase in wages and the necessity of joining together to create a union to obtain this particular demand. Three situations were discussed during the session, and the motif was always the same.

Now imagine an educator who has organized *his* educational program for these men, consisting of reading "wholesome" texts in which one learns that "the water is in the well" But precisely this type of thing happens all the time in both education and politics, because it is not realized that the dialogical nature of education begins with thematic investigation.

Once the decoding in the circles has been completed, the last stage of the investigation begins, as the investigators undertake a systematic interdisciplinary study of their findings. Listening to the tapes recorded during the decoding sessions and studying the notes taken by the psychologists and the sociologist, the investigators begin to list the themes explicit or implicit in the affirmations made during the sessions. These themes should be classified according to the various social sciences. Classification does not mean that when the program is elaborated the themes will be seen as belonging to isolated categories, but only that a theme is viewed in a specific manner by each of the social sciences to which it is related. The theme of development, for example, is especially appropriate to the field of economics, but not exclusively so. This theme would also be focalized by sociology, anthropology, and social psychology (fields concerned with cultural change and with the modification of attitudes and values — questions which are equally relevant to a philosophy of development).

It would be focalized by political science (a field concerned with the decisions which involve development), by education, and so forth. In this way, the themes which characterize a totality will never be approached rigidly. It would indeed be a pity if the themes, after being investigated in the richness of their interpenetration with other aspects of reality, were subsequently to be handled in such a way as to sacrifice their richness (and hence their force) to the strictures of specialties.

Once the thematic demarcation is completed, each specialist presents to the interdisciplinary team a project for the "breakdown" of his theme. In breaking down the theme, the specialist looks for the fundamental nuclei which, comprising learning units and establishing a sequence, give a general view of the theme. As each specific project is discussed, the other specialists make suggestions. These may be incorporated into the project and/or may be included in the brief essays to be written on the theme. These essays, to which bibliographic suggestions are annexed, are valuable aids in training the teacher-students who will work in the "culture circles."

During this effort to break down the meaningful thematics, the team will recognize the need to include some fundamental themes which were not directly suggested by the people during the preceding investigation. The introduction of these themes has proved to be necessary, and also corresponds to the dialogical character of education. If educational programming is dialogical, the teacher-students also have the right to participate by including themes not previously suggested. Call the latter type of theme "hinged themes," due to their function. They may either facilitate the connection between two themes in the program unit, filling a possible gap between the two; or they may illustrate the relations between the general program content and the view of the world held by the people. Hence, one of these themes may be located at the beginning of thematic units.

The anthropological concept of culture is one of these hinged themes. It clarifies the role of people' in the world and with the world as transforming rather than adaptive beings.

Once the breakdown of the thematics is completed, there follows the stage of its "codification": choosing the best channel of communication for each theme and its representation. A codification may be simple or compound. The former utilizes either the visual (pictorial or graphic), the tactile, or the auditive channel; the latter utilizes various channels. The selection of the pictorial or graphic channel depends not only on the material to be codified, but also on whether or not the individuals with whom one wishes to communicate are literate.

After the thematics has been codified, the didactic material (photographs, slides, film strips, posters, reading texts, and so forth) is prepared. The team may propose some themes or aspects of some themes to outside specialists as topics for recorded interviews.

Let us take the theme of development as an example. The team approaches two or more economists of varying schools of thought, tells them about the program, and invites them to contribute an interview on the subject in language comprehensible to the audience. If the specialists accept, an interview of fifteen to twenty minutes is taped. A photograph may be taken of each specialist while he is speaking.

When the taped interview is presented to the culture circle, an introductory statement indicates who each speaker is, what she or he has written, done, and doing now; meanwhile, the speaker's photograph is projected on a screen. If, for instance, the speaker is a university professor; the introduction could include a discussion regarding what the participants think of universities and what they expect of them. The group has already been told that the recorded interview will be followed by a discussion of its contents (which function as an auditive codification). The team subsequently reports to the specialist the reaction of the participants during the discussion. This technique links intellectuals, often well-intentioned but not infrequently alienated from the reality of the people, to that reality. It also gives the people an opportunity to hear and criticize the thought of intellectuals.

Some themes or nuclei may be presented by means of brief dramatizations, containing the theme only-no "solutions"! The dramatization acts as a codification, as a problem-posing situation to be discussed.

Another didactic resource — as long as it is carried out within a problem-posing rather than a banking approach to education — is the reading and discussion of magazine articles, newspapers, and book chapters (beginning with passages). As in the case of the recorded interviews, the author is introduced before the group begins, and the contents are discussed afterward.

Along the same lines, it is indispensable to analyze the contents of newspaper editorials following any given event: "why do different newspapers have such different interpretations of the same fact?" This practice helps develop a sense of criticism, so that people will react to newspapers or news broadcasts not as passive objects of the "communiques" directed at them, but rather as consciousnesses seeking to be free.

With all the didactic material prepared, to which should be added small introductory manuals, the team of educators is ready to represent to the people their own thematics, in systematized and amplified form. The thematics which have come from the people return to them-not as contents to be deposited, but as problems to be solved.

The first task of the basic-education teachers is to present the general program of the educational campaign. The people will find themselves in this program; it will not seem strange to them, since it originated with them. The educators will also explain (based on the dialogical character of education) the presence in the program of the hinged themes, and their significance.

If the educators lack sufficient funds to carry out the preliminary thematic investigation as described above, they can — with a minimum knowledge of the situation — select some basic themes to serve as "codifications to be investigated." Accordingly they can begin with introductory themes and simultaneously initiate further thematic investigation.

One of these basic themes is the anthropological concept of culture. Whether men and women are peasants or urban workers, learning to read or enrolled in a post-literacy program, the starting point of their search to know more (in the instrumental meaning of the term) is the debate of the concept. As they discuss the world of culture, they express their level of awareness of reality in which various themes are implicit. Their discussion touches upon other aspects of reality which comes to be perceived in an increasingly critical manner These aspects in turn involve many other themes.

With the experience now behind me, the concept of culture, discussed imaginatively in all or most of its dimensions, can provide various aspects of an educational program. One of the group members may say; for example: "I'd like to talk about nationalism."

"Very well," says the educator, noting down the suggestion, and adds: "what does nationalism mean? Why is a discussion about nationalism of any interest to us?" When a suggestion is posed as a problem to the group, new themes appear. If, in an area where (for example) thirty culture circles meet on the same night, all the "co-ordinators" (educators) proceed in this fashion, the central team will have a rich variety of thematic material for study.

The important thing, from the point of view of libertarian education, is for the people to come to feel like masters of their thinking by discussing the thinking and views of the world explicitly or implicitly manifest in their own suggestions and those of their comrades. Because this view of education starts with the conviction that it cannot present its own program but must search for this program dialogically with the people, it serves to introduce the pedagogy of the oppressed, in the elaboration of which the oppressed must participate.

Authentic Assessment

Simply testing an isolated skill or a retained fact does not effectively measure a student's capabilities. To accurately evaluate what a person has learned, an assessment method must examine his or her collective abilities. This is what is meant by authentic assessment. Authentic assessment presents students with real-world challenges that require them to apply their relevant skills and knowledge.

Authentic assessment accomplishes each of the following goals:

— Requires students to develop responses rather than select from predetermined options

— Elicits higher order thinking in addition to basic skills

— Directly evaluates holistic projects

— Synthesizes with classroom instruction

— Uses samples of student work (portfolios) collected over an extended time period

— Stems from clear criteria made known to students

— Allows for the possibility of multiple human judgments

— Relates more closely to classroom learning

— Teaches students to evaluate their own work

"Fairness" does not exist when assessment is uniform, standardized, impersonal, and absolute. Rather, it exists when assessment is appropriate—in other words, when it's personalized, natural, and flexible; when it can be modified to pinpoint specific abilities and function at the relevant level of difficulty; and when it promotes a rapport between examiner and student.

Authentic assessment is designed to be criterion-referenced rather than norm-referenced. Such evaluation identifies strengths and weaknesses, but does not compare or rank students.

Authentic assessment is often based on performance: Students are asked to demonstrate their knowledge, skills, or competencies in whatever way they find appropriate.

There are several challenges to using authentic assessment methods. They include managing its time-intensive nature, ensuring curricular validity, and minimizing evaluator bias.

Classroom Assessment

Classroom Assessment Techniques consist of a variety of feedback and discussion methods that gauge the quality of the learning process.

Classroom Assessment Techniques (CATs), also known as Classroom Research or Action Research, are a series of tools and practices designed to give teachers accurate information about the quality of student learning. Information gathered isn't used for grading or teacher evaluation. Instead, it's used to facilitate dialogue between students and teacher on the quality of the learning process, and how to improve it. As authors Patricia Cross and Thomas Angelo state in their book *Classroom Assessment Techniques*, "Teaching without learning is just talking." CATs provide both teachers and students with "in process" information on how well students are learning what the curriculum intends.

The three basic questions CATs ask are:

— What are the essential skills and knowledge I am trying to teach?

— How can I find out whether students are learning them?

— How can I help students learn better?

The classroom assessment process assumes that students need to receive feedback early and often, that they need to evaluate the quality of their own learning, and that they can help the teacher improve the strength of instruction.

The basic steps in the classroom assessment process are:

— Choose a learning goal to assess

— Choose an assessment technique

— Apply the technique

— Analyse the data and share the results with students

— Respond to the data

CATs provide teachers with a "menu" of evaluation tools that:

— Check for student background knowledge
— Identify areas of confusion
— Enable students to self-assess their learning level
— Determine students' learning styles
— Target and build specific skills

Portfolio Assessment

Portfolio assessment provides a body of student work—essentially, a portfolio—that can be used to appraise student performance over time.

Portfolio assessment ranges from portfolios that demonstrates the student's best work to an "expanded student record" that holds a full representation of the student's work, from math equations to essays on literature. There has been some confusion in the field as to who the portfolio is being kept for. For example, in some cases, student portfolios serve as a replacement for the high school diploma or transcript.

The disadvantage of portfolios is that they're not as quick and easy to evaluate, plus they're hard to rank, as with a grade or score. Because portfolios are qualitative, many employers find them difficult to use as a determinant of a candidate's skills. Often, employers would rather see a quantitative demonstration of a student's best skills and work.

Some schools create portfolios that serve as a representative sample of a student's work, showing the range of performance and experience. Such records usually hold far more information that employers need. Other schools want to use portfolios as an assessment tool to provide an alternative to standardized or teacher testing.

In some schools there has been much discussion on who "owns" the portfolio, the student or the school?

Ownership implies who gets to decide what goes into the portfolio, where the portfolio is stored, and what happens to the portfolio after graduation.

Let's look the implications portfolios have on the following elements of education:

— *Curriculum*: Some people believe that using portfolios will enable teachers to broaden their curriculum to include areas they traditionally could not assess with standardized testing. How well this works depends on how much a curriculum is developed "to the test," in other words, how much curriculum is geared towards achieving high test scores rather than learning for learning's sake.

— *Instruction*: Portfolio assessment appears to compliment a teacher's use of instructional strategies centered around teamwork, projects, and applied learning. Portfolios are also compatible with more individualized instruction, as well as strategies focused on different learning styles.

— *Assessment*: A portfolio can be used as an assessment tool. External assessors—employers, evaluation panels, and so on—can benefit from them. Teachers can also utilize them to judge student performance. Plus, students can use their own portfolios for self-assessment and reflectio

7

Philosophy of Liberal and Vocational Learning

Despite the fact that hardly anyone since Socrates has seriously held that it is possible to settle interesting philosophical problems by establishing strict definitions, the drawing of significant conceptual *distinctions* is arguably still the main stock-in-trade of professional philosophers. The trouble is, however, that since conceptual distinctions are apt to atrophy in the form of dualisms on the one hand, or are liable to generate problem cases on the other, it is also not uncommon to encounter attitudes of some distrust and hostility among philosophers towards distinction making.

While in contemporary mainstream philosophy, the day-to-day business of fine distinction-making continues unabated among philosophers, it is also true that numerous traditional distinctions, enshrining what many have come to regard as unacceptable dualisms, have come under heavy fire in recent times.

One particularly good example of this philosophical iconoclasm is the assault mounted by philosophers broadly located in the pragmatist tradition on the empiricist distinction between the *analytic* and the *synthetic* — a distinction nowadays commonly denounced as useless for any significant practical philosophical purpose.

Yet it is also possible to argue, as other contemporary philosophers have shown, that it is not that the analytic-synthetic distinction serves no real philosophical purpose but that its purpose has been obscured by the failure of past philosophers to separate it from other quite different distinctions — between the *necessary* and the *contingent*, the *a priori* and the *a posteriori*, and so on. From this perspective, the real problem might well be not that a distinction has been drawn for no good purpose, but that insufficient distinctions have been drawn in circumstances where there are actually grounds for several.

The arguments of this paper rest on the conviction that there are in fact closely parallel instances in the sphere of educational philosophy and that the common distinction between liberal and vocational learning is a particularly good case in point. Indeed, the distinction between the liberal and the vocational was considerably reinforced in the heyday of analytical philosophy of education when educational philosophers such as Richard Peters and Israel Scheffler first applied the tools of conceptual analysis to the confusions and muddles of educational discourse and distinction making was very much the order of the day.

Many of those distinctions and the dualisms to which they gave rise, however, have lately come under serious attack from those who follow in the pragmatist and deeply anti-dualist tradition of John Dewey and, unsurprisingly, the distinction between liberal and vocational education has been a principal target.

One problem of major theoretical and practical proportions which continues to dog educational theorists and policy makers is that of curriculum differentiation.

Essentially this is the difficulty of devising an appropriate content for education — a program of variously valued knowledge and skills — which is apt for distribution over a given population of learners heterogeneous with regard to individual differences of ability, aptitude, interest, values, aspirations, social circumstance, cultural background and so forth.

In particular, of course, this is a pressing problem for state-maintained systems of schooling which are charged — in the name of some overall conception of social justice — with providing something like a common and equal educational experience for all.

The problem usually surfaces at two main levels — at the level of individual needs and at that of social requirements. First, then, the problem may be seen as one of what it is right and proper to do in terms of the best educational interests of the individual.

On the one hand, it seems *prima facie* fair that all children should be afforded opportunity of access to all the recognized benefits of education and unfair that any child should be denied exposure to any part of what is generally acknowledged to be of educational value; on the other hand, however, it also seems unfair that some children should be required to persist in the learning of that for which they have little taste or aptitude — and it seems, on evidence, that the academically oriented curriculum of traditional liberal education affords not inconsiderable difficulties for the many non-academically minded citizens of most human societies.

But, secondly, the problem also has economic, social and political dimensions in the context of state maintained education since it is rightly supposed that schooling exists not merely for the benefit of the individual but also for the common good; thus, it may well seem of importance to provide students with precisely those learning experiences which will best equip them for the occupational lives they are destined to lead after school.

From this perspective, however unfair it may appear to limit the academic experience of certain non-academically inclined children, it is clearly wasteful of national and social resources — as well as against their personal inclinations — to require their initiation into academic disciplines which do not interest them to the exclusion of practical and vocational subjects which do and which also contribute to meeting the urgent needs of industry, service and commerce.

A Plethora of Distinctions

It would be tedious to recount the full history of this issue and the various strategies which have been suggested over the course of two millennia[3] to address it. Historically, it probably assumes urgent significance during the nineteenth century in debates in Britain and other western European cultures about the character and content of mass popular education — precisely in the light of explicit attempts by philosophers and social theorists to formulate a distinction between academic or liberal education and vocational preparation.

In particular, the issue loomed large in relation to the elaborate psychometric program of the first half of the twentieth century which culminated in the U.K. in the separate provision of different kinds of education for allegedly different intellectual categories of children on the basis of academic selection at eleven years of age. However, analogues of the liberal-vocational distinction invariably bedevil debates surrounding educational policy making in most developed societies. They continue to turn up, for example, in the interminable wrangles between conservatives and elitists, who are invariably sympathetic to alternative schooling and curricula for different sorts of children, and liberals and egalitarians who argue, on the basis of this or that notion of justice, for a common curriculum as the right of everyone.

However, the very fact that the debates and issues in question are liable to be characterized in a wide variety of ways, considered alongside the generally unilluminating nature of their outcomes, should alert us to the possibility that perhaps rather *different* questions are at issue here, so that the way to wisdom regarding the true problem might lie through distinguishing more clearly what the relevant questions are. From this point of view, Richard Pring, in a number of important recent publications, gets off to an excellent start in his own treatment of these issues both by way of his general perception of the urgent need for some basic conceptual geography in this area and in his recognition that a substantial amount of confusion may have been engendered by the illegitimate conflation of a set of rather *different* distinctions.

These include, for example, education and training, theory and practice, the academic and the vocational and what is of intrinsic rather than instrumental value. However, it is disappointing that having insightfully recognized the pressing need for better conceptual geography in this area, Professor Pring seems, by and large.

Indeed, the strategy to which Pring seems inclined is the more familiar one of denouncing these distinctions in favor of some kind of pragmatic reconciliation or resolution of them. Indeed, he directly invokes the authority of John Dewey, that great archenemy of philosophical dualisms, in this connection. The problems engendered by the liberal-vocational dichotomy may disappear if only that theory is implicit in intelligent practice, that training can also be educational, that vocational activities can be pursued for their own sake, and so on. But whilst all this may well be true it can also be doubted whether any significant dualism *is* resolved by these considerations — apart, that is, from the illegitimate one which follows from the wrongful conflation of different and separate distinctions; indeed, Pring is himself forced to fall back on a serious use of the distinctions in order to make the points that vocational training *can* be educational, theory *can* be inherent in practice and so forth.

For the truth is that the distinctions which Pring and others seem to want to blur in the interests of resolving awkward philosophical or educational dualisms have significant implications for our understanding of the function of schooling in relation to the proper educational and other development of young people. As such, they are not so easily disposed of by this casual sleight of hand.

Hence, although it may be true that vocational training *can* be pursued for its own sake, it is also important to recognize that there are other non-instrumentally valuable goals which have negligible vocational implications and to which rightly feel that *all* children should have access. And whilst it may be true that practical learning is at least as important for many purposes as academic learning it is also arguable that at the heart of *education* lie certain forms of understanding which are in an important sense inherently theoretical or academic to the significant exclusion of the practical.

Schooling and Education

The liberal-vocational dichotomy rather differently, by firmly putting asunder what Pring and others show a strong inclination to conjoin. A useful way into this issue is to recognize that these different distinctions can serve a range of significant conceptual purposes, and that the proper task is to explore the implications for a coherent account of education and schooling of the complex ways in which they overlap and interrelate.

When the matter is addressed in this way what emerges is a more fine-grained picture of the relationship between education and schooling and of the function and purpose of the latter in relation to individual and social flourishing than seems hitherto to have been recognized. Moreover, while there are all sorts of philosophical, political and practical reasons why people may be reluctant to embrace this more complex picture there can be little doubt that much error and confusion inevitably follows from a failure to do so.

The former interpretation, of course, construes the practical aspects of learning an academic discipline as only a *means* to understanding it more effectively and it is quite compatible with observing a sharp distinction between education and vocational training. The second interpretation, however, sees education as available just *as much* through practical and vocational pursuits as through traditional academic disciplines and is compatible with the view that for some children vocational learning may provide a legitimate alternative to or substitute for the learning of traditional subjects.

However, this seriously confuses the issue to the extent that it suggests this improved conception of vocationalism might for some children count as an education which is in some substantial sense the equivalent of what their more academic peers will be getting through the traditional educational disciplines. For no matter how principled one might try to make an initiation into hairdressing skills it is patently disingenuous to suggest that this might provide some sort of educational substitute for disinterested non-vocational development of a young person's understanding of his own culture and traditions.

The principal failure here, of course, is to distinguish between two quite different issues and considerations — that of whether properly providing children with the right sort of *education* and that of whether properly preparing young people for a life of work beyond school.

This issue is confused on a well nigh cosmic scale in arguments between what one might call *instrumentalists* and *non-instrumentalists* about the nature of education and schooling; the former claim that the main purpose of schooling (which they regard as synonymous with education) is to prepare young people for the adult life of post-school work and social relationships and the latter insist that education (which they regard as synonymous with schooling) is exclusively concerned with the initiation of children into those intrinsically valuable forms of knowledge which can assist them to understand their own personal, cultural or universal predicament.

The proper way out of this impasse, of course, is to recognize that although the instrumentalist is largely right to assert what he does of schooling and the non-instrumentalist is quite correct about education; both of them would be quite wrong if they put matters the other way around. In short it would *not* be true to say that education is primarily about equipping young people with life skills or that schooling is exclusively about the initiation of individuals into a personal understanding of themselves and the world for its own sake.

In short, the instrumentalist confuses education with schooling and the non-instrumentalist confuses schooling with education. However, that schooling (which is a social institution) and education (which is not) are conceptually separate (albeit practically related) enterprises and that education is only *one* of the many purposes of schooling then the problem is not so much of seeing how vocationalism might be made educational or education vocationalized but of how to do justice to both education *and* vocational training within a coherent overall conception of the diverse purposes of institutionalized schooling.

Distinctions and Dualisms

To acknowledge that in relation to the school curriculum there is room for the claims of both instrumentalists and non-instrumentalists is essentially to recognize that it is proper for people to require quite different benefits from the experience of schooling and that there are therefore quite different reasons for including various subjects and activities in the conventional state curriculum. Thus, one can hardly deny that human agents do require both theory and practice for the successful pursuit of their projects; they do engage in activities and pursuits for their own sake as well as for instrumental reasons; and they require, in the interests of a more general education, some initiation into a personal appreciation of what is worth living for as well as some of the vocationally useful skills which might assist them to earn their living.

These distinctions are by no means identical, as Pring himself observes, but it is precisely on this account that each of them is necessary for a clear understanding of education and schooling; they interrelate and cut across each other in markedly different ways in diverse curriculum subjects and activities and they serve to identify the various purposes for which different activities are standardly included in school curricula.

The important and philosophically urgent task of exploring in full detail the precise educational significance of each of these distinctions and of tracing the exact pattern of their many interesting interrelationships. However, although R. S. Peters is arguably the most culpable of modern educational philosophers and theorists with regard to his own quite blatant conflation of all the distinctions under consideration, his work nonetheless provides a useful starting point for thinking clearly about the general logical geography of this area.

To be sure, there are certain regrettable dualist tendencies in Peters's thought — clearly apparent in his exclusive identification of education with intellectual reflection, his denial that practice has much to contribute to a principled understanding of the world, and that practices have anything more than instrumental value, and so forth — which call for proper philosophical resistance.

Thus, while in the course of recognizing that education concerns the acquisition of knowledge and understanding that knowledge has its practical as well as theoretical aspects, wise to bear in mind that not all sorts of knowledge are centrally implicated in educational development. As Peters argued, education concerns the acquisition of the sort of knowledge which is capable of affording a broad intellectual and explanatory perspective on the world and one's place in it, rather than the mere know how of practical skills.

Of course, practice may indeed serve or contribute to the promotion of such explanation and understanding in precisely the way that scientific experiment can contribute to scientific knowledge or the movements of the dancer express the meaning of the dance; but the practical skills of experiment or dance are by no means self-explanatory and it is not hard to see how they might well be acquired in the absence of real understanding. Again, various sports and games may well be performed only for their own sake if that means for no other purpose than the sheer enjoyment of them, but this certainly does not mean that they are educational ends in themselves in the way that history or science are; for whereas rational reflection on nature or inquiry into the human past are well nigh paradigm cases of what it means to have one's understanding of the world substantially enlarged, it is less plausible to claim that hockey or netball contribute comparably to any educated appreciation of the human natural, cultural or social predicament.

This is certainly not an attempt to downgrade the non-educational aspects of human development or to argue that practices and skills of negligible educational significance have no legitimate place in the school curriculum. For although such practices and skills may have little to contribute to the educational development of an individual (however much their performance may entail the grasp of practical rational principles) they may yet play an indispensable part in schooling with regard to programs of vocational training, so-called leisure education and elsewhere.

What should be apparent from all this, of course, is that although any human activity or enterprise whatsoever can be viewed as having theoretical *and* practical aspects, as amenable to study in *either* academic *or* vocational terms or as pursuable for its own sake *or* as a means to an end, it is above all crucial to see why, in the light of these distinctions and some coherent conception of the aims of schooling and education, a range of diverse school subjects have traditionally been included in the school curriculum.

What seldom seems to be done with regard to so-called curriculum theory, however, is precisely to consider the various possible reasons for teaching this or that subject in its particularity rather than as part of some general story about what school subjects ought to be contributing to the educational or other development of pupils.

Hence, the familiar non-instrumentalist account of the school curriculum canvassed by the new liberal educational philosophers of the sixties tended to assume, or was often taken to assume, that for a subject to be worthy of curricular inclusion it must be shown to have genuine educational value. Likewise, some subsequent officially prescribed curricula would seem to imply that for a subject to be considered worthwhile, it must be susceptible to instrumental justification by reference to various extrinsic economic, social or political benefits.

Generally, the route to more light than heat regarding the liberal-vocational debate lies neither through the construction of largely rhetorical arguments in favor of one side or the other nor through some deliberate blurring of significant differences between the two. Instead what is needed is more attention to what particular school subjects or forms of knowledge have in their quite distinctive ways to contribute to the human development of young people, consistent with ensuring that their due entitlement to education *and* various forms of training is not unfairly unequal where it should be equal or unfairly equal where it need not be so.

To start with, in response to vocationalist skepticism about the value of academic subjects we could ask whether we might ever decently propose that we should dispense in the context of schooling — at least in the case of some children — with their substantial initiation into the sorts of activities which non-instrumentalists argue to be of intrinsic educational value, such as science, history, literature, art and mathematics. These, of course, are precisely the forms of knowledge and understanding which liberal educationalists insist that no one should be denied access to if they are to become civilized and rational members of society. Put thus, however, it should be clear from what has been said so far that we are here faced with several categories of educational activity rather than just one.

As regards history and literature, for example, we are clearly dealing with activities which have genuine intrinsic value from an educational point of view but practically negligible utility or instrumental value.However, that despite this — indeed, precisely on account of the crucial contribution that history and literature have to make to the education of civilized sensibilities — most reflective people would wish to maintain that in general the more children know about history and literature, to the best of their abilities, the better.

When it comes to the various forms of scientific study, of course, we are faced with activities which have *both* educational and instrumental value in view of their contribution to our understanding of the natural circumstances of human life *and* their obvious technological implications for and applications to a wide range of problems which may also have vocational import for the future of many children in schools. For various reasons we cannot fully explore here, however, it is arguable that substantial scientific understanding is not as crucial as substantial understanding of history for the development of an educated appreciation of their cultural identity on the part of *all* children, and so a proper strategy might be to go for a minimum of general science for everyone and more vocationally oriented specialist programs of pure and applied science for those whose particular abilities and interests take them in that direction.

Non-instrumentalists, of course, make much of the intrinsic educational value of mathematics and of its being concerned with considerably more than the promotion of mere numeracy. But again beware of assuming that because it is possible to make sense of mathematics as an intrinsically worthwhile form of human understanding it is thereby appropriate to teach it as such to *all* children; for if mathematics is also an activity for which a certain natural flair or ability is required — as has often been maintained — then it may well be that mathematical *education* can never be a realistic option, as it would be hard to claim of history, for those who lack the necessary intellectual requirements.

In that case we may have to accept that it is no more realistic to entertain any substantial degree of mathematical understanding as a valid goal of educational development for all children than it is to entertain musical appreciation and performance as educational goals for those on whom nature has bestowed a so-called tin ear. But to recognize that a serious conceptual understanding of mathematics is beyond the reach of very many children is quite consistent with endorsing a strong instrumentalist line on the importance of a thorough school training for all in basic mathematical skills on the common sense grounds that basic numeracy is an urgent requirement for the day to day practical purposes of all members of society.

What has already been said in relation to music would also seem to apply to painting and dance and to many other arts for which a particular flair is required; whilst there is room here for an initiation into the basics, particularly at the primary level, it would seem that a freedom to choose according to ability or interests should enter the picture fairly soon at the secondary stage of education. A distinction which might be of considerable significance here, of course, is that between appreciation and participation in these art forms since it would appear to make sense to try to promote appreciation on a rather wider scale than training in the actual skills of performance. Once again, however, it seems possible to conclude on the basis of common experience that whilst there are considerations and circumstances of physical or other kinds which might interfere with a person's appreciation of either music or painting there are also no arguments here of the sort to which we might appeal on behalf of the indispensable educational benefits of literature for requiring the exposure of *all* children to other fine arts.

It is also likely that there are no compelling educational grounds for requiring the initiation of children into certain physical sports and games — although there may be valid reasons, if these are empirically sustainable, for including such activities in the school curriculum on the extrinsic grounds of their potential for the promotion of health and fitness. But arguments based on the alleged value of such activities for the development of moral, spiritual or aesthetic understanding or appreciation are at best highly contested and more than likely simply confused.

A little, to conclude this very truncated survey of the content of the conventional school curriculum, about the value of a whole range of kinds of knowledge and skill of a primarily instrumental nature — domestic, craft, and technical skills of various kinds. Here again, the relevant distinction may well be between the basic skills of everyday coping such as elementary home economics, computing or woodwork, to which it is reasonable to introduce *everyone* to some degree, and such higher specialist vocational competencies as electronic engineering or commercial and business skills which may be relevant only to those who wish to pursue eventual careers in such areas.

To be sure, each of these observations stands in need of considerably more by way of detailed and substantial argument; my main point is that the overall tendency of the argument should not be in the direction of some general ideological defense of *either* liberal education *or* vocational preparation *or* of some dubious resolution of the two, but towards a better recognition and appreciation of what the various distinctions which underlie what some have seen as an unacceptable dualism have to reveal about the structure and complexity of human needs and interests and the capacity and potential of both schooling and education to satisfy them. Young people do not need secretarial skills or business studies *instead* of history or biology; in at least some cases (but not all) they require *both*.

Again, they may not need electronics if they have no wish to pursue a technological career and it may not be necessary to require their initiation into the conceptual complexities of mathematical understanding if they have no recognizable aptitude for it. On the other hand they do require the skills of numeracy even if they have trouble mastering them and some substantial knowledge and appreciation of history, geography and literature irrespective of whether they have any real taste for such studies.

My argument has been, then, that a serious exploration of the conceptual geography of the various distinctions which underlie the vexed dichotomy of liberal versus vocational education might help us to appreciate rather better what a given subject, form of knowledge or activity is actually *for* in the context of schooling. Precisely, it might assist us to appreciate, in terms which are more rational than dogmatic, the distinctive contribution that a given activity may have to make to some aspect of the development of persons in a way which enables us to recognize and respect both their human individuality as well as their important moral and cultural kinship with others.

8

Pedagogy for Teachers

Over the last 30 years or so, there has been a strong response by critical theorists to traditional public school ideology. With the advent of progressive British schools of thought and subsequent American responses, which viewed schools as forms of social control, to critical ethnographic studies which described how schools merely mirrored social class distinctions, to other social issues that depicted schools as enclaves of race, class and gender inequity, critical pedagogy as a concept and resulting practices has arisen as a form of thought and action to challenge the dominant and oppressive ideologies contructed historically, for our purposes, around public school concerns.

As a form of social action, there has been much criticism leveled against critical pedagogues and critical pedagogy. These criticisms revolve around at least three central themes:

— What right do critical pedagogues have to speak for the oppressed and marginalized, particularly when "speaking" comes out of a middle class university or other teaching position.

— The language used by critical pedagogues is so opaque that the average teacher cannot understand some basic critical,' premises made. This would contradict the basic message of challenging forms of oppression, subordination and domination. What's more, the language itself becomes a form of domination!

— Critical pedagogy is theoretically visionary but lacks the practical tools to accompany it.

The above three criticisms are poignant. On a very simple level I could answer these claims in this manner:

— Any one has a right to struggle for democracy, from whatever social class position one is situated in. As long as the intent is for social justice, then who cares.

— While the language is opaque, don't we as a new social movement have to create a new and vibrant language to challenge old forms of language and therefore thinking?

— A part of critical pedagogy IS to struggle against formulaic enterprises. One cannot be practical in the traditional sense because every context and reality differs. In other words, one cannot give the "ten" steps for a critical pedagogy, especially if critical pedagogy differs in different arenas.

Schooling and Education

Critical pedagogy roots itself in the belief that every citizen deserves an education. The distinction between schooling and education is important here. Given the structure of schools, in which a socially efficient system of management and control is in place (rigid rule structure, standardized curriculum, etc.), schools often forget about the role of an educated person and rely more on what I term "schooling" methods to secure a future for students. Schooling has a number of components to it. The basic logic for schooling relies on preparing students for a market economy. And, this logic is fuelled by many national education reports, both past and present. This form of reasoning is also exacerbated both in and out of schools—parents signifying to their children that what is needed for a better job is an education, tracking systems in school that in hidden ways prepare students for differentiated social class divisions, excessive competition to prepare students for the economy (SAT scores and other standardized tests) and a market logic of the survival of the fittest mentality.

Underneath this rubric of market logic lies the students need to be purely extrinsically motivated to learn. Grades, pop quizzes, fear of their results, cheating systems, reward structures that filter a immediate gratification logic, strict accountability models for teachers, demeaning stereotyping, sterile teaching methodologies, rote learning, forgetting information the next day or simply after a test, and the like, place the student and teacher in the awful predicament of using schooling as a socialization mechanism that loses sight of the many reasons for attending schools in the first place—nurture, care, community, citizenship preparation—in short, a broad education.

One would be remiss to suggest that schooling and all its implications, both positive and negative, isn't an important element (and at times needed) of any child's structure. I would, for example, want my child to receive schooling so as to attain a good paying job. But, the promise of the enlightenment doesn't reside in schooling. It simply resides in receiving an education.

Education presupposes intrinsic motivation—that the student is intrinsically motivated to learn and the teacher intrinsically motivated to teach. While grades and the like are an important element to school structures, the reason for teaching and learning are not fuelled by numbers—but by a sheer desire to attain knowledge for knowledge sake.

Put differently, an education in public schools as well as in the higher academy involves passion for one's subject matter, the ability to get student to think critically, being creative about subject matter content, creating a classroom of an active community revolved around the learning of material, and the strong desire to teach and to learn. Above all else, education involves the teacher understanding the schooling structure that wouldn't allow education to ensue. Thus, the ability to create an education involves the understanding of schooling mechanisms.

Challenging its very presuppositions, particularly its negatives, means becoming a transformative intellectual—-and that is for both teachers as well as students. Put another way, to educate rather than school is to resist the very base of school value structures. On the one hand, creating transformative intellectuals means being critical of all forms of schooling.

On the other hand, being a transformative intellectual puts the teacher into a moral bind. What kind of education can I give my students that can create a space for them so as they can be critical citizens, so I can generate democracy in my classrooms, so I can open up options for them, given the pervasiveness and need for schooling to survive in this country?

It seems to me that many reasons teachers want to become teachers is because they desire to educate their students. But, as they enter into the system, often times they are led to "school" their clientele, much like they were schooled both in their public school history as well as their teacher education departments. The following dichotomies discusses schooling and education from different angles, citing examples of how we presently do both.

Control Versus Democracy

Under the guise of schooling, schools become control mechanisms. On many levels, this contradicts the message of democracy that we believe America is supposedly all about. Comments Purpel :

> Schools have been captured by the concept of accountability, which has been transformed from a notion that schools need to be responsive and responsible to community concerns to one in which numbers are used to demonstrate that schools have met their minimal requirements—a reductionism which has given priority to the need to control than to understand educational considerations. The need to control produces control mechanisms, and for schools this has meant a proliferation of tests a kind of quality control mechanism borrowed crudely and inappropriately from certain industrial settings. We control the curriculum, teachers and staff by insisting on predefined minimal performances on specified tests... in this case it means metaphors like efficiency, cost-effectiveness, quality control, production... obsession with control also gets expressed in school policy on Discipline," an interesting term which transfers to gain control over behaviour.

Even further than Purpel suggests, the issue of control is compounded when schools control the way we act, feel and think. Control of ideas, values and stereotypes (race, class and gender), often exacerbated by media culture, are portrayed in schools in no uncertain terms. Simply put, schooling at its worst here, is the replication and/or the promotion of these stereotypes as forms of control mechanisms. Additionally, "schooling" will under the guise of "control," determine social class through standardized testing, create national reports to support these tests (read Nation at Risk), presuppose that to control by extending homework and a longer school day will automatically lead to an education and so on.

Under the guise of education, democracy rears its head. Here, control mechanisms are challenged, negotiated and subverted. That does not mean, for instance, that one has to abandon testing. This is a necessary evil in an economically driven country. One has to, however, realize that public schools have been historically charged with the responsibility to sustain and promote democratic principles. Such school curricula as social studies, citizenship classes, humanity courses, and government and history classes are a critical outlet for these democratic principles. However, critical pedagogy holds that democratic principles must become a way of life in all subject areas and all extra-curricular content—be they pedagogically demonstrated in math, science and other content areas.

One doesn't have to be a social science teacher to challenge control mechanisms. Examples would include teachers and students in all subject areas creating limits for behaviour control by writing class rules co-operatively, and teachers and students negotiating forms of testing, other than taking the regular rote, standardized type only.

Democratic education also involves fostering a challenge to all forms of individualism and negative competition—two principles that brush against the grain of civic participation. More co-operative learning, less stress on the value of "success" as the major reason for coming to school, and more individual student participation in written, verbal or math projects will allow for the possibility of student voices to be heard. Perhaps most importantly, an educated teacher and student works within the schooling control mechanisms' boundaries. For example, a critical pedagogue teacher striving for a democratic education will seek to test democratically, negotiate curriculum with administrators and students where appropriate and work within school rules to create a just and fair system.

The issue of control and democracy is an on-going and perplexing dichotomy. More democracy is better than less. And, under the guise of an "education," a critical pedagogue will strive to democratize her/his class as a part of a broader vision for students and the school she/he is teaching in. As a part of this schooling and education complexity I turn to issues of authoritarianism and authority.

Authoritarianism Versus Authority

Within a "schooling" mind-set, control mechanisms, a standardized curriculum, a rigid rule structure, and top-down hierarchy guide the authoritarian nature of schools. Authoritarianism, thus defined, rears its head in a bureaucratic system. Within this authoritarian structure, clearly defined structural leaders and their subordinates form a hierarchical ladder of control and division of labour (teacher tasks, various male or female related student tasks, division of principal and vice-principal tasks, predominant male principals and female vice-principals, etc.). This notion of authoritarianism is embedded in what schools like to believe as "authority." It is usually defined rigidly and unwaveringly. My argument here is not to abandon school structure, but rather to redefine this structure in what I have termed, "educated" ways. Thus, the turn to authority.

A critical pedagogue will seek education first by understanding that "authority" has multiple meanings and can be democratically negotiated. First, the teacher "educator" is an authority over his/her subject matter. Second, the teacher "educator" is not the only authority in the classroom. Teachers and students share each other's knowledge. Learning this way becomes reciprocal and dialogical. That is, teachers learn as well—in particular about student cultures. In other words, students become authorities over their own cultures. As an example, for a white male or female to teach successfully in the inner city, he or she would have to understand and respect the cultural diversity of all students.

Third, teachers can use their authority to create relationships that would enhance education—relationships of caring and nurturing—relationships that challenge schooling notions of oppressive race, class and gender stereotypes. Teacher "educators" can be in charge of how students relate to race, class and gender seating arrangements, language construction in the class, and the abolition of stereotypes. These are just a few examples of how under the guise of "authority" schooling authoritarianism can be challenged.

Teachers as "educators" will also use authority to open avenues to negotiate differences. Superseding the schooling aspect of authoritarianism and control, and under this rubric of authority and education, teachers will explore multiple avenues in which authority can be redefined in the name of establishing social relationships that are not only democratic, but life sustaining and possessing the possibility of opening spaces for "authority" in one's personal and public life.

In classrooms, this necessarily means that critical pedagogues interested in "educating" begin to interpret history from multiple ethnic perspectives, allowing literature to take on a life of its own, situated contextually within the life of the student as well as history! In Math this may mean equating economics and social relationships as a form of living rather than only rigid formula as authoritatively the only correct avenue to knowledge. Problem solving must begin to redefine teachers as authorities for a meaningful education, one that has the potential not only of challenging authoritarian teaching techniques, but of also undermining the worst of schooling.

Individualism Versus Individuality

The progressive "educator," much like the transformative

intellectual, possesses the ability to "see" through various oppressive school structures. For instance, the critical pedagogue clearly envisions how schools promote the value of individualism over individuality. On a simple note, individualism signifies the quest for human supremacy, excessive and at times negative forms of competition, self and instant gratification, and narcissism. Here, the belief is that the individual is the center of life. A sort of survival of the fittest mentality fits this theme.

The quest for individual material goods (commodities, wealth, grades, etc) becomes a part of this school structure. What this translates itself into: Standardized tests and the division of social class, the set-up of a reward system that merely promotes swashbuckling competition between peers, stereotypes based on one's personal achievement, gender bias, basing one's worth on achievement, gifted programs, honour roll societies, stickers, university entrance exams, school cheating systems and merit systems that promote individual antagonism, etc.

My argument here is that we cannot avoid the individualism trap all the time. Schooling is a part of individualism. But, we CAN challenge it where necessary. As critical pedagogues, teachers will realize that individualism at its worst will breed contempt, even though it seems like a necessary evil in this economically driven society.

One way, however, to challenge the above form of reasoning, is to fall back on a simple but profound understanding as to why most teachers became teachers in the first place, before they experience burn out—love kids, want to help, want to make a difference, etc. Simply to "love" or make a difference is not enough in the big picture, particularly if one begins to align with critical pedagogy.

The educated and "critical" teacher will acknowledge individual accomplishments, base one's worth on who one is rather than what one accomplishes, listen to and empathize with a student voice' by both understanding student heritage and history and by being critical of one's own history. Typically, some individuals may flourish better in groups. The critically minded teacher who is to educate will understand that structurally there will always be tension between individual and group accomplishment and individual and group worth.

The educated teacher, the one disposed to resist individualism, will search for multiple avenues of "authentic" assessment, varying forms of discipline, alternate rule making, divergent forms of classroom management, and will challenge students to think of community, not only selfishly, etc. This "critical" teacher will "open up" in teacher meetings by subtly challenging peers to view what is being done via school policy as promoting an often damaging ethic of competition.

This is not to say that critical pedagogues should challenge every policy, but that the right times and spots must be chosen to seek the common good, the ethical responses to forms of the alienation, subordination and oppression that individualism breeds. To me, the best form of resistance to individualism is the "living out" of individuality—the ability to walk the walk and talk the talk.

As critical educators, it seems imperative that we find borders of understanding with other individuals who are not on the same ideological path. If progressive changes are to be made, this notion of individuality will have to be harnessed. To deny voices of ideological opposition, for instance, while noble, is still to contradict the very premise of individuality. After all, the essence of democracy is the promotion of the individuality that is so often suppressed by school structures.

De-skilling Versus Re-skilling

The "schooled" teacher is deskilled. That is, teachers lack control over their own work. For instance, a deskilled teacher doesn't make curricular decisions, and even if she/he does, doesn't really seriously investigate why certain decisions are made. Deskilling has to do with teachers executing someone else's goals and plans. In industry, this is referred to as the separation of conception from execution. In school this appears as well.

Pre-service teachers are taught the skills to teach—to execute tasks, manage the classroom, develop discipline procedures, create assignments, make tests, evaluate tests, disseminate curriculum, build unit plans, and vary teaching methodologies. Ironically, this works in ways to deskill teachers. This happens when the skills teachers are taught in teacher education are unusable in practice, such as in highly populated minority or/and urban areas.

Deskilling is at its peak when teachers lack autonomy over teaching and decision making processes. By making teachers accountable for state-mandated curriculum (such as basal reading materials) and by promoting competency-based education, system management, and employing rigid and dehumanizing forms of evaluation along with numerical rating scales, teachers are controlled and simply march to the tune of the state.

An educated teacher, a critical pedagogue in the making, fully understands and feels this deskilling process. The notion of reskilling occurs when teachers are both aware and critical of the multiple forms of deskilling. Reskilling occurs when teachers challenge stereotyping, find ways to subvert tracking through alternative teaching methodologies, build curriculum with open and critical spirits, become engrossed in policy-oriented decisions of the state and local school district sites, and form common understandings over issues of value.

In short, reskilling occurs when teachers are able to move around forms of schooling, and ultimately find ways to educate. Acts of reflection on subject matter, on short and long term goals of "educational" transformation as well as searching for those values that challenge forms of personal and institutional oppression will serve the educated and critical teacher well. On the practical side, this means that if social studies teachers are to teach about the tenets of democracy, democratic practice must occur in the classroom. Or, if Literature teachers are to teach Hamlet, then "to be or not to be" is an identity issue that must be grappled with the students in the context of student lives, not only Hamlets'.

Math teachers would have to concretize math problems in the context of student lives, with the intent to "reskill" students as well, not get them to be mere robots of formulas and the like. Art must speak to student lives, as would reading and writing. Practically, teachers would have to get students to literally "get over" stereotypes and begin to create exercises that promote empathy. In short, the educator turned critical pedagogue becomes a reskilled practitioner—committed to justice particularly within the confines of the schooling structure.

Traditional Literacy Versus Critical Literacy

Under the schooling rubric, traditional literacy holds schools morally accountable to f provide a technical mastery of skills for students; to be functional in the basics of reading, math, and writing. More than that, "schooling" or traditional literacy also means teaching the above functions on multiple levels (say, 4th, 6th, 9th, or 12th grades), but with little creativity, no sense of purpose other than to go on to the next grade, and little moral vision or insight as to a larger picture revolving around "education."

Critical literacy under the guise of education distinguishes itself from the above literacy in that it begs teachers to teach for analytical purposes, for multiple interpretations, for moral reasoning. Under critical literacy, the educated teacher, as well as student, takes issues such as gender, class and race seriously both in classroom management as well as curriculum content. Critical literacy allows the teacher to connect curriculum to texts as well as to student experience, thus making knowledge more relevant and introspective for both teacher and student. For example, a critically literate teacher will always reskill her/himself by asking if History can be read from multiple ethnic perspectives.

The critical math teacher will connect economics and problem solving to student experiences. The critical social studies teacher will always strive for democracy, be critical over the civil war by connecting content to present communities, racial divides and so on. In short, the critical literate teacher under an educated mind-set, while certainly "schooling" her/his students in the technical sense (getting facts straight, partaking in standardized tests, etc.), adds a necessary clause to their teaching portfolio. There is a committed and visionary understanding that critical pedagogy is a form of education that must be strived for as necessary acts of resistance to oppressive schooling structures!

9

Marxist Philosophy of Education

While the problem of humanization has always, from an axiological point of view, been humankind's central problem, it now takes on the character of an inescapable concern. Concern for humanization leads at once to the recognition of dehumanization, not only as an ontological possibility but as an historical reality And as an individual perceives the extent of dehumanization, he or she may ask if humanization is a viable possibility. Within history in concrete, objective contexts, both humanization and dehumanization are possibilities for a person as an uncompleted being conscious of their incompletion.

But while both humanization and dehumanization are real alternatives, only the first is the people's vocation. This vocation is constantly negated, yet it is affirmed by that very negation. It is thwarted by injustice, exploitation, oppression, and the violence of the oppressors; it is affirmed by the yearning of the oppressed for freedom and justice, and by their struggle to recover their lost humanity.

Dehumanization, which marks not only those whose humanity has been stolen, but also (though in a different way) those who have stolen it, is a *distortion* of the vocation of becoming more fully human. This distortion occurs within history; but it is not an historical vocation. Indeed, to admit of dehumanization as an historical vocation would lead either to cynicism or total despair. The struggle for humanization, for the emancipation of labor, for the overcoming of alienation, for the affirmation of men and women as persons would be meaningless. This struggle is possible only because dehumanization, although a concrete historical fact, is *not* a given destiny but the result of an unjust order that engenders violence in the oppressors, which in turn dehumanizes the oppressed.

Because it is a distortion of being more fully human, sooner or later being less human leads the oppressed to struggle against those who made them so. In order for this struggle to have meaning, the oppressed must not in seeking to regain their humanity (which is a way to create it), become in turn oppressors of the oppressors, but rather restorers of the humanity of both.

This, then, is the great humanistic and historical task of the oppressed: to liberate themselves and their oppressors as well. The oppressors, who oppress, exploit, and rape by virtue of their power; cannot find in this power the strength to liberate either the oppressed or themselves. Only power that springs from the weakness of the oppressed will be sufficiently strong to free both. Any attempt to "soften" the power of the oppressor in deference to the weakness of the oppressed almost always manifests itself in the form of false generosity; indeed, the attempt never goes beyond this. In order to have the continued opportunity to express their "generosity," the oppressors must perpetuate injustice as well. An unjust social order is the permanent fount of this "generosity" which is nourished by death, despair, and poverty. That is why the dispensers of false generosity become desperate at the slightest threat to its source.

True generosity consists precisely in fighting to destroy the causes which nourish false charity. False charity constrains the fearful and subdued, the "rejects of life" to extend their trembling hands. True generosity lies in striving so that these hands — whether of individuals or entire peoples — need be extended less and less in supplication, so that more and more they become human hands which work and, working, transform the world.

This lesson and this apprenticeship must come, however, from the oppressed themselves and from those who are truly in solidarity with them. As individuals or as peoples, by fighting for the restoration of their humanity they will be attempting the restoration of true generosity. Who are better prepared than the oppressed to understand the terrible significance of an oppressive society? Who suffer the effects of oppression more than the oppressed? Who can better understand the necessity of liberation? They will not gain this liberation by chance but through the praxis of their quest for it, through their recognition of the necessity to fight for it. And this fight, because of the purpose given it by the oppressed, will actually constitute an act of love opposing the lovelessness. which lies at the heart of the oppressors' violence, lovelessness even when clothed in false generosity.

But almost always, during the initial stage of the struggle, the oppressed, instead of striving for liberation, tend themselves to become oppressors, or "sub-oppressors." The very structure of their thought has been conditioned by the contradictions of the concrete, existential situation by which they were shaped. Their ideal is to be men; but for them, to be men is to be oppressors. This is their model of humanity. This phenomenon derives from the fact that the oppressed, at a certain moment of their existential experience, adopt an attitude of "adhesion" to the oppressor. Under these circumstances they cannot "consider" him sufficiently clearly to objectivize him — to discover him "outside" themselves. This does not necessarily mean that the oppressed are unaware that they are downtrodden. But their perception of themselves as oppressed is impaired by their submersion in the reality of oppression. At this level, their perception of themselves as opposites of the oppressor does not yet signify engagement in a struggle to overcome the contradiction; the one pole aspires not to liberation, but to identification with its opposite pole.

In this situation the oppressed do not see the "new man as the person to be born from the resolution of this contradiction, as oppression gives way to liberation. For them, the new man or woman themselves become oppressors. Their vision of the new man or woman is individualistic; because of their identification with the oppressor they have no consciousness of themselves as persons or as members of an oppressed class. It is not to become free that they want agrarian reform, but in order to acquire land and thus become landowners — or; more precisely, bosses over other workers.

It is a rare peasant who, once "promoted" to overseer, does not become more of a tyrant towards his former comrades than the owner himself. This is because the context of the peasant's situation, that is, oppression, remains unchanged. In this example, the overseer, in order to make sure of his job, must be as tough as the owner — and more so. Thus is illustrated our previous assertion that during the initial stage of their struggle the oppressed find in the oppressor their model of "manhood."

Even revolution, which transforms a concrete situation of oppression by establishing the process of liberation, must confront thus phenomenon. Many of the oppressed who directly or indirectly participate in revolution intend — conditioned by the myths of the old order — to make it their private revolution. The shadow of their former oppressor is still cast over them.

The "fear of freedom" which afflicts the oppressed, a fear which may equally well lead them to desire the role of oppressor or bind them to the role of oppressed, should be examined. One of the basic elements of the relationship between oppressor and oppressed is *prescription.* Every prescription represents the imposition of one individual's choice upon another, transforming the consciousness of the person prescribed to into one that conforms with the prescriber's consciousness. Thus, the behavior of the oppressed is a prescribed behavior, following as it does the guidelines of the oppressor.

The oppressed, having internalized the image of the oppressor and adopted his guidelines, are fearful of freedom. Freedom would require them to eject this image and replace it with autonomy and responsibility. Freedom is acquired by conquest, not by gift. It must be pursued constantly and responsibly. Freedom is not an ideal located outside of man; nor is it an idea which becomes myth. It is rather the indispensable condition for the quest for human completion.

To surmount the situation of oppression, people must first critically recognize its causes, so that through transforming action they can create a new situation, one which makes possible the pursuit of a fuller humanity. But the struggle to be more fully human has already begun in the authentic struggle to transform the situation. Although the situation of oppression is a dehumanized and dehumanizing totality affecting both the oppressors and those whom they oppress, it is the latter who must, from their stifled humanity, wage for both the struggle for a fuller humanity; the oppressor, who is himself dehumanized because he dehumanizes others, is unable to lead this struggle.

However, the oppressed, who have adapted to the structure of domination in which they are immersed, and have become resigned to it, are inhibited from waging the struggle for freedom so long as they feel incapable of running the risks it requires. Moreover, their struggle for freedom threatens not only the oppressor, but also their own oppressed comrades who are fearful of still greater repression.

When they discover within themselves the yearning to be free, they perceive that this yearning can be transformed into reality only when the same yearning is aroused in their comrades. But while dominated by the fear of freedom they refuse to appeal to others, or to listen to the appeals of others, or even to the appeals of their own conscience. They prefer gregariousness to authentic comradeship; they prefer the security of conformity with their state of unfreedom to the creative communion produced by freedom and even the very pursuit of freedom.

The oppressed suffer from the duality which has established itself in their innermost being. They discover that without freedom they cannot exist authentically. Yet, although they desire authentic existence, they fear it. They are at one and the same time themselves and the oppressor whose consciousness they have internalized.

The conflict lies in the choice between being wholly themselves or being divided; between ejecting the oppressor within or not ejecting them; between human solidarity or alienation; between following prescriptions or having choices; between being spectators or actors; between acting or having the illusion of acting through the action of the oppressors; between speaking out or being silent, castrated in their power to create and re-create, in their power to transform the world. This is the tragic dilemma of the oppressed which their education must take into account.

This book will present some aspects of what the writer has termed the pedagogy of the oppressed, a pedagogy which must be forged *with*, not for, the oppressed (whether individuals or peoples) in the incessant struggle to regain their humanity. This pedagogy makes oppression and its causes objects of reflection by the oppressed, and from that reflection will come their necessary engagement in the struggle for their liberation. And in the struggle this pedagogy will be made and remade.

The central problem is this: How can the oppressed, as divided, unauthentic beings, participate in developing the pedagogy of their liberation? Only as they discover themselves to be "hosts" of the oppressor can they contribute to the midwifery of their liberating pedagogy. As long as they live in the duality in which *to be* is *to be like*, and *to be like* is *to be like the oppressor*, this contribution is impossible. The pedagogy of the oppressed is an instrument for their critical discovery that both they and their oppressors are manifestations of dehumanization.

Liberation is thus a childbirth, and a painful one. The man or woman who emerges is a new person, viable only as the oppressor-oppressed contradiction is superseded by the humanization of all people. Or to put it another way the solution of this contradiction is born in the labor which brings into the world this new being: no longer oppressor nor longer oppressed, but human in the process of achieving freedom.

This solution cannot be achieved in idealistic terms. In order for the oppressed to be able to wage the struggle for their liberation they must perceive the reality of oppression not as a closed world from which there is no exit, but as a limiting situation which they can transform. This perception is a necessary but not a sufficient condition for liberation; it must become the motivating force for liberating action. Nor does the discovery by the oppressed that they exist in dialectical relationship to the oppressor, as his antithesis that without them the oppressor could not exist— in itself constitute liberation. The oppressed can overcome the contradiction in which they are caught only when this perception enlists them in the struggle to free themselves.

The same is true with respect to the individual oppressor as person. Discovering himself to be an oppressor may cause considerable anguish, but it does not necessarily lead to solidarity with the oppressed. Rationalizing his guilt through paternalistic treatment of the oppressed, all the while holding them fast in a position of dependence, will not do. Solidarity requires that one enter into the situation of those with whom one is in solidarity; it is a radical posture. If what characterizes the oppressed is their subordination to the consciousness of the master, as Hegel affirms, true solidarity with the oppressed means fighting at their side to transform the objective reality which has made them these "beings for another".

The oppressor is in solidarity with the oppressed only when he stops regarding the oppressed as an abstract category and sees them as persons who have been unjustly dealt with, deprived of their voice, cheated in the sale of their labor — when he stops making pious, sentimental, and individualistic gestures and risks an act of love. True solidarity is found only in the plenitude of this act of love, in its existentiality in its praxis. To affirm that men and women are persons and as persons should be free, and yet to do nothing tangible to make this affirmation a reality, is a farce.

Since it is a concrete situation that the oppressor-oppressed contradiction is established, the resolution of this contradiction must be *objectively* verifiable. Hence, the radical requirement — both for the individual who discovers himself or herself to be an oppressor and for the oppressed — that the concrete situation which begets oppression must be transformed.

To present this radical demand for the objective transformation of reality to combat subjectivist immobility which would divert the recognition of oppression into patient waiting for oppression to disappear by itself is not to dismiss the role of subjectivity in the struggle to change structures. On the contrary one cannot conceive of objectivity without subjectivity. Neither can exist without the other, nor can they be dichotomized.

The separation of objectivity from subjectivity, the denial of the latter when analyzing reality or acting upon it, is objectivism. On the other hand, the denial of objectivity in analysis or action, resulting in a subjectivism which leads to solipsistic positions, denies action itself by denying objective reality. Neither objectivism nor subjectivism, nor yet psychologism is propounded here, but rather subjectivity and objectivity in constant dialectical relationship.

To deny the importance of subjectivity in the process of transforming the world and history is naive and simplistic. It is to admit the impossible: a world without people. This objectivistic position is as ingenuous as that of subjectivism, which postulates people without a world. World and human beings do not exist apart from each other, they exist in constant interaction. Man does not espouse such a dichotomy; nor does any other critical, realistic thinker. What Marx criticized and scientifically destroyed was not subjectivity, but subjectivism and psychologism. Just as objective social reality exists not by chance, but as the product of human action, so it is not transformed by chance. If humankind produce social reality (which in the "inversion of the praxis" turns back upon them and conditions them), then transforming that reality is an historical task, a task for humanity.

Reality which becomes oppressive results in the contradistinction of men as oppressors and oppressed The latter, whose task it is to struggle for their liberation together with those who show true solidarity, must acquire a critical awareness of oppression through the praxis of this struggle. One of the gravest obstacles to the achievement of liberation is that oppressive reality absorbs those within it and thereby acts to submerge human beings' consiousness. Functionally, oppression is domesticating. To no longer be prey to its force, one must emerge from it and turn upon it. This can be done only by means of the praxis: reflection and action upon the world in order to transform it.

Hay que hacer al opresion real todavia mas opresiva anadiendo a aquella la *conciencia* de la opresion haciendo la infamia todavia mas infamante, al pregonarla.

Making "real oppression more oppressive still by adding to it the realization of oppression" corresponds to the dialectical relation between the subjective and the objective. Only in this interdependence is an authentic praxis possible, without which it is impossible to resolve the oppressor-oppressed contradiction. To achieve this goal, the oppressed must confront reality critically, simultaneously objectifying and acting upon that reality. A mere perception of reality not followed by this critical intervention will not lead to a transformation of objective reality — precisely because it is not a true perception. This is the case of a purely subjectivist perception by someone who forsakes objective reality and creates a false substitute.

A different type of false perception occurs when a change in objective reality would threaten the individual or class interests of the perceiver. In the first instance, there is no critical intervention in reality because that reality is fictitious; there is none in the second instance because intervention would contradict the class interests of the perceiver In the latter case the tendency of the perceiver is to behave "neurotically."

The fact exists; but both the fact and what may result from it may be prejudicial to the person. Thus it becomes necessary not precisely to deny the fact, but to "see it differently." This rationalization as a defense mechanism coincides in the end with subjectivism. A fact which is not denied but whose truths are rationalized loses its objective base. It ceases to be concrete and becomes a myth created in defense of the class of the perceiver.

Herein lies one of the reasons for the prohibitions and the difficulties designed to dissuade the people from critical intervention in reality. The oppressor knows full well that this intervention would not be to his interest. What is to his interest is for the people to continue in a state of submersion, impotent in the face of oppressive reality. Of relevance here is Lukacs' warning to the revolutionary party: ... il doit, pour employer les mots de Marx, expliquer aux masses leur propre action non seulement afin d'assurer la continuite des experiences revolutionnaires du proletariat, mais aussi d'activer consciemment le developpement ulterieur de ces experiences.

In affirming this necessity, Lukacs is unquestionably posing the problem of critical intervention. "To explain to the masses their own action" is to clarify and illuminate that action, both regarding its relationship to the objective acts by which it was prompted, and regarding its purposes. The more the people unveil this challenging reality which is to be the object of their transforming action, the more critically they enter that reality. In this way they are "consciously activating the subsequent development of their experiences." There would be no human action if there were no objective reality; no world to be the "not I" of the person and to challenge them; just as there would be no human action if humankind were not a "project" if he or she were not able to transcend himself or herself, if one were not able to perceive reality and understand it in order to transform it.

In dialectical thought, world and action are intimately interdependent. But action is human only when it is not merely an occupation but also a preoccupation, that is, when it is not dichotomized from reflection. Reflection, which is essential to action, is implicit in Lukacs' requirement of "explaining to the masses their own action," just as it is implicit in the purpose he attributes to this explanation: that of "consciously activating the subsequent development of experience."

For us, however, the requirement is seen not in terms of explaining to, but rather dialoguing with the people about their actions. In any event, no reality transforms itself, and the duty which Lukacs ascribes to the revolutionary party of "explaining to the masses their own action" coincides with our affirmation of the need for the critical intervention of the people in reality through the praxis. The pedagogy of the oppressed, which is the pedagogy of people engaged in the fight for their own liberation, has its roots here. And those who recognize, or begin to recognize, themselves as oppressed must be among the developers of this pedagogy. No pedagogy which is truly liberating can remain distant from the oppressed by treating them as unfortunates and by presenting for their emulation models from among the oppressors. The oppressed must be their own example in the struggle for their redemption.

The pedagogy of the oppressed, animated by authentic, humanist (not humanitarian) generosity, presents itself as a pedagogy of humankind. Pedagogy which begins with the egoistic interests of the oppressors (an egoism cloaked in the false generosity of paternalism) and makes of the oppressed the objects of its humanitarianism, itself maintains and embodies oppression. It is an instrument of dehumanization. This is why, as we affirmed earlier, the pedagogy of the oppressed cannot be developed or practiced by the oppressor. It would be a contradiction in terms if the oppressors not only defended but actually implemented a liberating education.

The pedagogy of the oppressed, as a humanist and libertarian pedagogy, has two distinct stages. In the first, the oppressed unveil the world of oppression and through the praxis commit themselves to its transformation. In the second stage, in which the reality of oppression has already been transformed, this pedagogy ceases to belong to the oppressed and becomes a pedagogy of all people in the process of permanent liberation.

In both stages, it is always through action in depth that the culture of domination is culturally confronted. In the first stage this confrontation occurs through the change in the way the oppressed perceive the world of oppression; in the second stage, through the expulsion of the myths created and developed in the old order, which like specters haunt the new structure emerging from the revolutionary transformation.

The pedagogy of the first stage must deal with the problem of the oppressed consciousness and the oppressor consciousness, the problem of men and women who oppress and men and women who suffer oppression. It must take into account their behavior; their view of the world, and their ethics. A particular problem is the duality of the oppressed: they are contradictory, divided beings, shaped by and existing in a concrete situation of oppression and violence.

Any situation in which "A" objectively exploits "B" or hinders his and her pursuit of self-affirmation as a responsible person is one of oppression. Such a situation in itself constitutes violence even when sweetened by false generosity; because it interferes with the individual's ontological and historical vocation to be more fully human. With the establishment of a relationship of oppression, violence has *already* begun. Never in history has violence been initiated by the oppressed. How could they be the initiators, if they themselves are the result of violence? How could they be the sponsors of something whose objective inauguration called forth their existence as oppressed? There would be no oppressed had there been no prior situation of violence to establish their subjugation.

Violence is initiated by those who oppress, who exploit, who fail to recognize others as persons — not by those who are oppressed, exploited, and unrecognized. It is not the unloved who initiate disaffection, but those who cannot love because they love only themselves. It is not the helpless, subject to terror, who initiate terror, but the violent, who with their power create the concrete situation which begets the "rejects of life." It is not the tyrannized who initiate despotism, but the tyrants. It is not the despised who initiate hatred, but those who despise. It is not those whose humanity is denied them who negate humankind, but those who denied that humanity (thus negating their own as well). Force is used not by those who have become weak under the preponderance of the strong, but by the strong who have emasculated them.

For the oppressors, however, it is always the oppressed (whom they obviously never call "the oppressed" but — depending on whether they are fellow countrymen or not — "those people" or "the blind and envious masses" or "savages" or "natives" or "subversives") who are disaffected, who are "violent," "barbaric," "wicked," or "ferocious" when they react to the violence of the oppressors.

Yet it is — paradoxical though it may seem — precisely in the response of the oppressed to the violence of their oppressors that a gesture of love may be found. Consciously or unconsciously, the act of rebellion by the oppressed (an act which is always, or nearly always, as violent as the initial violence of the oppressors) can initiate love.

Whereas the violence of the oppressors prevents the oppressed from being fully human, the response of the latter to this violence is grounded in the desire to pursue the right to be human. As the oppressors dehumanize others and violate their rights, they themselves also become dehumanized. As the oppressed, fighting to be human, take away the oppressors' power to dominate and suppress, they restore to the oppressors the humanity they had lost in the exercise of oppression.

It is only the oppressed who, by freeing themselves, can free their oppressors. The latter, as an oppressive class, can free neither others nor themselves. It is therefore essential that the oppressed wage the struggle to resolve the contradiction in which they are caught; and the contradiction will be resolved by the appearance of the new man: neither oppressor nor oppressed, but man in the process of liberation. If the goal of the oppressed is to become fully human, they will not achieve their goal by merely reversing the terms of the contradiction, by simply changing poles.

This may seem simplistic; it is not. Resolution of the oppressor-oppressed contradiction indeed implies the disappearance of the oppressors as a dominant class. However, the restraints imposed by the former oppressed on their oppressors, so that the latter cannot reassume their former position, do not constitute *oppression.* An act is oppressive only when it prevents people from being more fully human. Accordingly, these necessary restraints do not *in themselves* signify that yesterday's oppressed have become today's oppressors. Acts which prevent the restoration of the oppressive regime cannot be compared with those which create and maintain it, cannot be compared with those by which a few men and women deny the majority the right to be human.

However, the moment the new regime hardens into a dominating "bureaucracy"_the humanist dimension of the struggle is lost and it is no longer possible to speak of liberation. Hence our insistence that the authentic solution of the oppressor-oppressed contradiction does not lie in a mere reversal of position, in moving from one pole to the other. Nor does it lie in the replacement of the former oppressors with new ones who continue to subjugate the oppressed — all in the name of their liberation.

But even when the contradiction is resolved authentically by a new situation established by the liberated laborers, the former oppressors do not feel liberated. On the contrary, they genuinely consider themselves to be oppressed. Conditioned by the experience of oppressing others, any situation other than their former seems to them like oppression. Formerly, they could eat, dress, wear shoes, be educated, travel, and hear Beethoven; while millions did not eat, had no clothes or shoes, neither studied nor traveled, much less listened to Beethoven.

Any restriction on this way of life, in the name of the rights of the community, appears to the former oppressors as a profound violation of their individual right — although they had no respect for the millions who suffered and died of hunger, pain, sorrow, and despair. For the oppressors, "human beings" refers only to themselves; other people are "things." For the oppressors, there exists only one right: their right to live in peace, over against the right, not always even recognized, but simply conceded, of the oppressed to survival. And they make this concession only because the existence of the oppressed is necessary to their own existence.

This behavior, this way of understanding the world and people (which necessarily makes the oppressors resist the installation of a new regime) is explained by their experience as a dominant class. Once a situation of violence and oppression has been established, it engenders an entire way of life and behavior for those caught up in it — oppressors and oppressed alike. Both are submerged in this situation, and both bear the marks of oppression.

Analysis of existential situations of oppression reveals that their inception lay in an act of violence — initiated by those with power. This violence, as a process, is perpetuated from generation to generation of oppressors, who become its heirs and are shaped in its climate. This climate creates in the oppressor a strongly possessive consciousness — possessive of the world and of men and women. Apart from direct, concrete, material possession of the world and of people, the oppressor consciousness could not understand itself — could not even exist. Fromm said of this consciousness that, without such possession, "it would lose contact with the world" The oppressor consciousness tends to transform everything surrounding it into an object of its domination. The earth, property, production, the creations of people, people themselves, time — everything is reduced to the status of objects at its disposal.

In their unrestrained eagerness to possess, the oppressors develop the conviction that it is possible for them to transform everything into objects of their purchasing power; hence their strictly materialistic concept of existence. Money is the measure of all things, and profit the primary goal. For the oppressors, what is worthwhile is to have more — always more — even at the cost of the oppressed having less or having nothing. For them, *to be* is *to have* and to be the class of the "haves."

As beneficiaries of a situation of oppression, the oppressors cannot perceive that if *having* is a condition of *being,* it is a necessary condition for all women and men. This is why their generosity is false. Humanity is a "thing" and they possess it as an exclusive right, as inherited property. To the oppressor consciousness, the humanization of the "others," of the people, appears not as the pursuit of full humanity; but as subversion.

The oppressors do not perceive their monopoly on *having more* as a privilege which dehumanizes others and themselves. They cannot see that, in the egoistic pursuit of *having* as a possessing class, they suffocate in their own possessions and no longer *are;* they merely *have.* For them, *having more* is an inalienable right, a right they acquired through their own "effort" with their "courage to take risks." If others do not have more, it is because they are incompetent and lazy; and worst of all is their unjustifiable ingratitude towards the "generous gestures" of the dominant class. Precisely because they are "ungrateful" and "envious," the oppressed are regarded as potential enemies who must be watched.

It could not he otherwise. If the humanization of the oppressed signifies subversion, so also does their freedom; hence the necessity for constant control. And the more the oppressors control the oppressed, the more they change them into apparently inanimate "things." This tendency of the oppressor consciousness to "in-animate" everything and everyone it encounters, in its eagerness to possess, unquestionably corresponds with a tendency to sadism.

The pleasure in complete domination over another person (or other animate creature) is the very essence of the sadistic drive. Another way of formulating the same thought is to say that the aim of sadism is to transform a man into a thing, something animate into something inanimate, since by complete and absolute control the living loses one essential quality of life — freedom.

Sadistic love is a perverted love — a love of death, not of life. One of the characteristics of the oppressor consciousness and its necrophilic view of the world is thus sadism. As the oppressor consciousness, in order to dominate, tries to deter the drive to search, the restlessness, and the creative power which characterize life, it kills life. More and more, the oppressors are using science and technology as unquestionably powerful instruments for their purpose: the maintenance of the oppressive order through manipulation and repression. The oppressed, as objects, as "things," have no purposes except those their oppressors prescribe for them.

Given the preceding context, another issue of indubitable importance arises: the fact that certain members of the oppressor class join the oppressed in their struggle for liberation, thus moving from one pole of the contradiction to the other. Theirs is a fundamental role, and has been so throughout the history of this struggle. It happens, however, that as they cease to be exploiters or indifferent spectators or simply the heirs of exploitation and move to the side of the exploited, they almost always bring with them the marks of their origin: their prejudices and their deformations, which include a lack of confidence in the people's ability to think, to want, and to know.

Accordingly these adherents to the people's cause constantly run the risk of falling into a type of generosity as malefic as that of the oppressors. The generosity of the oppressors is nourished by an unjust order, which must be maintained in order to justify that generosity. Our converts, on the other hand, truly desire to transform the unjust order; but because of their background they believe that they must be the executors of the transformation. They talk about the people, but they do not trust them; and trusting the people is the indispensable precondition for revolutionary change. A real humanist can be identified more by his trust in the people, which engages him in their struggle, than by a thousand actions in their favor without that trust.

Those who authentically commit themselves to the people must re-examine themselves constantly. This conversion is so radical as not to allow of ambiguous behavior. To affirm this commitment but to consider oneself the proprietor of revolutionary wisdom — which must then be given to (or imposed on) the people — is to retain the old ways. The man or woman who proclaims devotion to the cause of liberation yet is unable to enter into *communion* with the people, whom he or she continues to regard as totally ignorant, is grievously self-deceived. The convert who approaches the people but feels alarm at each step they take, each doubt they express, and each suggestion they offer; and attempts to impose his "status", remains nostalgic towards his origins.

Conversion to the people requires a profound rebirth. Those who undergo it must take on a new form of existence; they can no longer remain as they were. Only through comradeship with the oppressed can the converts understand their characteristic ways of living and behaving, which in diverse moments reflect the structure of domination. One of these characteristics is the previously mentioned existential duality of the oppressed, who are at the same time themselves and the oppressor whose image they have internalized. Accordingly, until they concretely "discover" their oppressor and in turn their own consciousness, they nearly always express fatalistic attitudes towards their situation.

The peasant begins to get courage to overcome his dependence when he realizes that he is dependent. Until then, he goes along with the boss and says "what can I do? I'm only a peasant."

When superficially analyzed, this fatalism is sometimes interpreted as a docility that is a trait of national character. Fatalism in the guise of docility is the fruit of an historical and sociological situation, not an essential characteristic of a people's behavior. It almost always is related to the power of destiny or fate or fortune — inevitable forces — or to a distorted view of God. Under the sway of magic and myth, the oppressed (especially the peasants, who are almost submerged in nature) see their suffering, the fruit of exploitation, as the will of God, as if God were the creator of this "organized disorder."

Submerged in reality, the oppressed cannot perceive clearly the "order" which serves the interests of the oppressors whose image they have internalized. Chafing under the restrictions of this order, they often manifest a type of horizontal violence, striking out at their own comrades for the pettiest reasons.

The colonized man will first manifest this aggressiveness which has been deposited in his bones against his own people. This is the period when the niggers beat each other up, and the police and magistrates do not know which way to turn when faced with the astonishing waves of crime in North Africa.... While the settler or the policeman has the right the livelong day to strike the native, to insult him and to make him crawl to them, you will see the native reaching for his knife at the slightest hostile or aggressive glance cast on him by another native; for the last resort of the native is to defend his personality vis-a-vis his brother.

It is possible that in this behavior they are once more manifesting their duality. Because the oppressor exists within their oppressed comrades, when they attack those comrades they are indirectly attacking the oppressor as well.

On the other hand, at a certain point in their existential experience the oppressed feel an irresistible attraction towards the oppressors and their way of life. Sharing this way of life becomes an overpowering aspiration. In their alienation, the oppressed want at any cost to resemble the oppressors, to imitate them, to follow them. This phenomenon is especially prevalent in the middle-class oppressed, who yearn to be equal to the "eminent" men and women of the upper class. Albert Memmi, in an exceptional analysis of the "colonized mentality," refers to the contempt he felt towards the colonizer, mixed with "passionate" attraction towards him.

How could the colonizer look after his workers while periodically gunning down a crowd of colonized?

How could the colonized deny himself so cruelly yet make such excessive demands? How could he hate the colonizers and yet admire them so passionately?

Self-depreciation is another characteristic of the oppressed, which derives from their internalization of the opinion the oppressors hold of them. So often do they hear that they are good for nothing, know nothing and are incapable of learning anything — that they are sick, lazy, and unproductive — that in the end they become convinced of their own unfitness.

The peasant feels inferior to the boss because the boss seems to be the only one who knows things and is able to run things.

They call themselves ignorant and say the "professor" is the one who has knowledge and to whom they should listen. The criteria of knowledge imposed upon them are the conventional ones. "Why don't you," said a peasant participating in a culture circle,"explain the pictures first? That way it'll take less time and won't give us a headache."

Almost never do they realize that they, too, "know things" they have learned in their relations with the world and with other women and men. Given the circumstances which have produced their duality, it is only natural that they distrust themselves.

Not infrequently, peasants in educational projects begin to discuss a generative theme in a lively manner, then stop suddenly and say to the educator: "Excuse us, we ought to keep quiet and let you talk. You are the one who knows, we don't know anything." They often insist that there is no difference between them and the animals; when they do admit a difference, it favors the animals. "They are freer than we are."

It is striking, however, to observe how this self-depreciation changes with the first changes in the situation of oppression. I heard a peasant leader say in an *asentamiento* meeting, "They used to say we were unproductive because we were lazy and drunkards. All lies. Now that we are respected as men, we're going to show everyone that we were never drunkards or lazy. We were exploited!"

As long as their ambiguity persists, the oppressed are reluctant to resist, and totally lack confidence in themselves. They have a diffuse, magical belief in the invulnerability and power of the oppressor._The magical force of the landowner's power holds particular sway in the rural areas. A sociologist friend of mine tells of a group of armed peasants in a Latin American country who recently took over a latifundium. For tactical reasons, they planned to hold the landowner as a hostage. But not one peasant had the courage to guard him; his very presence was terrifying. It is also possible that the act of opposing the boss provoked guilt feelings. In truth, the boss was "inside" them.

The oppressed must see examples of the vulnerability of the oppressor so that a contrary conviction can begin to grow within them. Until this occurs they will continue disheartened, fearful, and beaten. As long as the oppressed remain unaware of the causes of their condition, they fatalistically "accept" their exploitation. Further, they are apt to react in a passive and alienated manner when confronted with the necessity to struggle for their freedom and self-affirmation. Little by little, however, they tend to try out forms of rebellious action. In working towards liberation, one must neither lose sight of this passivity nor overlook the moment of awakening.

Within their unauthentic view of the world and of themselves, the oppressed feel like "things" owned by the oppressor. For the latter; *to be* is *to have,* almost always at the expense of those who have nothing. For the oppressed, at a certain point in their existential experience, *to be* is not to resemble the oppressor, but *to be under* him, to depend on him. Accordingly, the oppressed are emotionally dependent.

The peasant is a dependent. He can't say what he wants. Before he discovers his dependence, he suffers. He lets off steam at home, where he shouts at his children, beats them, and despairs. He complains about his wife and thinks everything is dreadful. He doesn't let off steam with the boss because he thinks the boss is a superior being. Lots of times, the peasant gives vent to his sorrows by drinking.

This total emotional dependence can lead the oppressed to what Fromm calls necrophilic behavior: the destruction of life — their own or that of their oppressed fellows.

It is only when the oppressed find the oppressor out and become involved in the organized struggle for their liberation that they begin to believe in themselves. This discovery cannot be purely intellectual but must involve action; nor can it be limited to mere activism, but must include serious reflection: only then will it be a praxis.

Critical and liberating dialogue, which presupposes action, must be carried on with the oppressed at whatever the stage of their struggle for liberation._The content of that dialogue can and should vary in accordance with historical conditions and the level at which the oppressed perceive reality. But to substitute monologue, slogans, and communiques for dialogue is to attempt to liberate the oppressed with the instruments of domestication. Attempting to liberate the oppressed without their reflective participation in the act of liberation is to treat them as objects which must be saved from a burning building; it is to lead them into the populist pitfall and transform them into masses which can be manipulated.

At all stages of their liberation, the oppressed must see themselves as women and men engaged in the ontological and historical vocation of becoming more fully human. Reflection and action become imperative when one does not erroneously attempt to dichotomize the content of humanity from its historical forms.

The insistence that the oppressed engage in reflection on their concrete situation is not a call to armchair revolution. On the contrary reflection — true reflection — leads to action. On the other hand, when the situation calls for action, that action will constitute an authentic praxis only if its consequences become the object of critical reflection. In this sense, the praxis is the new *raison d'être* of the oppressed; and the revolution, which inaugurates the historical moment of this *raison d'être,* is not viable apart from their concomitant conscious involvement. Otherwise, action is pure activism.

To achieve this praxis, however; it is necessary to trust in the oppressed and in their ability to reason. Whoever lacks this trust will fail to initiate (or will abandon) dialogue, reflection, and communication, and will fall into using slogans, communiques, monologues, and instructions. Superficial conversions to the cause of liberation carry this danger.

Political action on the side of the oppressed must be pedagogical action in the authentic sense of the word, and, therefore, action *with* the oppressed. Those who work for liberation must not take advantage of the emotional dependence of the oppressed — dependence that is the fruit of the concrete situation of domination which surrounds them and which engendered their unauthentic view of the world. Using their dependence to create still greater dependence is an oppressor tactic.

Libertarian action must recognize this dependence as a weak point and must attempt through reflection and action to transform it into independence. However, not even the best-intentioned leadership can bestow independence as a gift. The liberation of the oppressed is a liberation of women and men, not things. Accordingly while no one liberates himself by his own efforts alone, neither is he liberated by others. Liberation, a human phenomenon, cannot be achieved by semihumans. Any attempt to treat people as semihumans only dehumanizes them. When people are already dehumanized, due to the oppression they suffer; the process of their liberation must not employ the methods of dehumanization.

The correct method for a revolutionary leadership to employ in the task of liberation is, therefore, *not* "libertarian propaganda." Nor can the leadership merely "implant" in the oppressed a belief in freedom, thus thinking to win their trust. The correct method lies in dialogue. The conviction of the oppressed that they must fight for their liberation is not a gift bestowed by the revolutionary leadership, but the result of their own *conscientizacao.*

The revolutionary leaders must realize that their own conviction of the necessity for struggle (an indispensable dimension of revolutionary wisdom) was not given to them by anyone else — if it is authentic. This conviction cannot be packaged and sold; it is reached, rather, by means of a totality of reflection and action. Only the leaders' own involvement in reality; within an historical situation, led them to criticize this situation and to wish to change it.

Likewise, the oppressed (who do not commit themselves to the struggle unless they are convinced, and who, if they do not make such a commitment, withhold the indispensable conditions for this struggle) must reach this conviction as Subjects, not as objects. They also must intervene critically in the situation which surrounds them and whose mark they bear; propaganda cannot achieve this. While the conviction of the necessity for struggle (without which the struggle is unfeasible) is indispensable to the revolutionary leadership (indeed, it was this conviction which constituted that leadership), it is also necessary for the oppressed. It is necessary; that is, unless one intends to carry out the transformation *for* the oppressed rather than *with* them. It is my belief that only the latter form of transformation is valid.

The object in presenting these considerations is to defend the eminently pedagogical character of the revolution. The revolutionary leaders of every epoch who have affirmed that the oppressed must accept the struggle for their liberation — an obvious point — have also thereby implicitly recognized the pedagogical aspect of this struggle. Many of these leaders, however (perhaps due to natural and understandable biases against pedagogy), have ended up using the "educational" methods employed by the oppressor. They deny pedagogical action in the liberation process, but they use propaganda to convince.

It is essential for the oppressed to realize that when they accept the struggle for humanization they also accept, from that moment, their total responsibility for the struggle. They must realize that they are fighting not merely for freedom from hunger, but for... freedom to create and to construct, to wonder and to venture. Such freedom requires that the individual be active and responsible, not a slave or a well-fed cog in the machine.... It is not enough that men are not slaves; if social conditions further the existence of automatons, the result will not be love of life, but love of death.

The oppressed, who have been shaped by the death-affirming climate of oppression, must find through their struggle the way to life-affirming humanization, which does not lie *simply* in having more to eat (although it does involve having more to eat and cannot fail to include this aspect). The oppressed have been destroyed precisely because their situation has reduced them to things. In order to regain their humanity they must cease to be things and fight as men and women. This is a radical requirement. They cannot enter the struggle as objects in order *later* to become human beings.

The struggle begins with men's recognition that they have been destroyed. Propaganda, management, manipulation — all arms of domination — cannot be the instruments of their rehumanization. The only effective instrument is a humanizing pedagogy in which the revolutionary leadership establishes a permanent relationship of dialogue with the oppressed. In a humanizing pedagogy the method ceases to be an instrument by which the teachers (in this instance, the revolutionary leadership) can manipulate the students (in this instance, the oppressed), because it expresses the consciousness of the students themselves.

The method is, in fact, the external form of consciousness manifest in acts, which takes on the fundamental property of consciousness — its intentionality. The essence of consciousness is being with the world, and this behavior is permanent and unavoidable. Accordingly consciousness is in essence a 'way towards' something apart from itself outside itself, which surrounds it and which it apprehends by means of its ideational capacity. Consciousness is thus by definition a method, in the most general sense of the word.

A revolutionary leadership must accordingly practice *co-intentional* education. Teachers and students (leadership and people), co-intent on reality, are both Subjects, not only in the task of unveiling that reality and thereby coming to know it critically, but in the task of re-creating that knowledge. As they attain this knowledge of reality through common reflection and action, they discover themselves as its permanent re-creators. In this way, the presence of the oppressed in the struggle for their liberation will be what it should be: not pseudo-participation, but committed involvement.

10

Adolescence and Ethical Development

The problem of moral education is among those questions that are now undergoing a reassessment in psychology and in culture in the most decisive and most thorough-going fashion. The thousand-year link between morality and religion has been broken, and, under the force of analysis, morality is beginning to acquire an increasingly temporal character. It is now possible to establish beyond all reasonable doubt the experiential, temporal character of morality, and its dependence on historical and social conditions, and its class character.

Every nationality and every epoch, and likewise every class, possesses its own morality, which is always a product of social psychology. There is the morality of the Hottentot, who, it is said, responds when asked the question, "What do you consider to be good, and what do you consider to be bad?" by declaring, "Good is when I steal a wife; bad is when I'm robbed."

Moral concepts and ideas vary depending upon the social environment, and what is considered bad at one time and in one place, elsewhere might be considered the greatest of all virtues. And if there are any common feature in all these different manifestations of moral consciousness that can be identified, this is only because certain common elements shared by every human society were once part of the social order.

Thus, from the standpoint of social psychology, ethics must be looked upon as a certain form of social behavior that was established and evolved in the interests of the ruling class, and is different for different classes. This is why there has always existed a morality of the ruler and a morality of slaves, and this is why epochs characterized by crises have represented the greatest crises of morality.

It is said that in the schools of ancient Sparta, children were forced to wait upon a common table while the adults had their meals. A child had to steal something from the table, and he would be punished only if he couldn't do this, or only if he were caught red-handed. The moral lesson of this experiment was to steal and not get caught. Such an ideal was entirely conditioned by the Communist order of the closed aristocratic society of Sparta, in which concern for property did not constitute the standard of morality, in which stealing, therefore, was not considered a sin, but where force, craftiness, cunning, and composure constituted the ideal of all citizens of Sparta, and where the greatest sin was the inability to deceive someone else and to control one's emotions.

As in every school of thought, moral education here coincides entirely with the class morality which guides the school. In France, where special classes in ethics have been introduced and where there are textbooks of morality in use, the educational ideal consists in those bourgeois virtues which permeate the mind and soul of the French middle-class. In one French textbook on morality, for example, there are hardly any "ethical standards," according to M.M. Rubinshtein, and in their place thriftiness is exalted and bank books turned into the criterion of morality.

Such class ideals are inherent to all other systems of education. This was also the case in the pre-revolutionary secondary schools, which were constructed on authoritarian foundations, in which obedience was considered the ideal for the student, and the general goals of moral education were to educate a loyal subject or a hard-working official.

Now that the world has experienced the cleansing threat of social revolution, the very foundations of bourgeois morality are trembling, and it is very possible that in no other realm do we meet up with such shapeless and tenuous ideas as in the domain of ethical standards. All those rules of bourgeois morality, which were fully laden with hypocrisy and mendacity, have lost their meaning.

Bourgeois morality was compelled to be hypocritical, because it taught one thing and did another, because it was constructed at the juncture of class interests and, preaching the kingdom of God after death, implanted a kingdom of enslavers in the world. Lies and hypocrisy were the natural source of such a form of morality, and sanctimoniousness was its inevitable accompaniment. The child saw one thing out in the world and was told something else altogether, and all the school's endeavor was oriented towards reconciling this divergence between real life and morality in the child as effortlessly as possible.

The child either was unable to reconcile the two, or, if he was taught how to do so, he would become accustomed to viewing morality as a kind of social decorum that everyone had to observe, though this always entailed great effort, in fact, it was only through such effort that he could assume this point of view. The child's moral consciousness could be reduced to the convictions of Griboedov's chambermaid, i.e., that

"There's nothing wrong with sinning, just don't spread rumors."

The fear of moral retribution supplied the compulsory sanction for morality, in addition to public opinion, and, in his moral behavior, man was easily guided psychologically by the very same custodial rules – this you should not do, but that you may do – and usually guided himself in all his behavior in precisely this way.

One Russian philosopher was right, in this sense, to refer to these moral concepts as embodying a kind of "moral policeman," since the force of moral precepts was rooted in the compulsory and humiliating power of fear in the face of moral punishment and the pangs of conscience. There was a special morality of the strong and the weak, and just as in regard to external laws, so in regard to the laws of conscience, the weak would submit to them, and the strong would rebel against them and break these laws. In its revolt against bourgeois morality, European philosophy proclaimed the immorality of its own basic laws, and speaking through Nietsche's lips, declared itself to be beyond good and evil.

Shestov says that man's relation to the categorical imperative is just like the attitude of the Russian peasant towards that forest of tall trees which Peter the Great had forbidden to cut down. In both cases, there is the attraction of an entirely arbitrary deed, though the individual still confronts the fear of retribution and punishment, in the one case external and in the other case internal. The moral commandment, "do not kill," has always been understood in just this sense; that is, "do not kill, not because that's the wrong road to take, but because you yourself will die from the pangs of conscience." This, the internal contradiction of bourgeois morality, was exposed by Dostoyevskil in *Crime and*

Punishment. In Nietzsche's revolt, the overall negative critical work of his thinking, in its attack on bourgeois morality, had the force of a stick of dynamite, exploding the very foundations of Christian morality from within.

A new morality will be created once a new human society will have been created, but at that point it is likely that moral behavior will have been entirely dissolved into general forms of behavior. All of behavior in general will be moral, because there will be no basis whatsoever for any conflict between the behavior of one person and the behavior of society in general.

Here it is possible to take note only of several points that the pedagogics of moral behavior must deal with. Note, first, the negation of the absolute, supra-empirical roots of morality, or of any innate morality of feelings. From the psychological point of view, moral behavior, like everything else, arises *on the foundation* of innate and instinctive reactions, and evolves under the influence of the methodical effects of the environment. Without question, the foundation of moral feelings have to be sought in the instinctive sense of sympathy for another person, in social instincts, and in much else besides. As it comes into contact with every imaginable datum, concept, and phenomenon in the process of growth.

Hence the general conclusion that moral behavior is a form of behavior which is amenable to education through the social environment in exactly the same way as is everything else.

We should also bear in mind the uncertainty that now pervades morality. On the one hand, revolutionary boldness is needed, not a narrow-minded view of things, in order to discern what is happening, what is its genuine meaning, and to know how to reject all those prejudices which only recently everyone believed to be unshakeable moral tenets. All that is left of bourgeois morality, like the corrupt legacy of a previous life, all this must be swept clear out of our schools. On the other hand, however, there is a certain risk concealed in this impermanence of present-day morality, the risk that all moral restraint will be lifted and the child's behavior become entirely arbitrary.

Bear in mind that such utter amoralism, the complete absence of all restraining principles, will return us to those naive ideals where our natural instincts are pursued, which modern man can in no way agree with. We cannot agree to the blind pursuit of the demands of our instincts, because we know in advance that these demands were begotten by previous epochs, and are the residue of the long-past experience of adaptation to vanished environmental conditions, and, consequently, pull us back, rather than carry us forward. Moreover, that the instincts must inevitably be restricted to, and adapt to new conditions in the world, constitutes the essential condition of education.

Consequently, within that uncertain chaos which the present-day state of morality presents, there are a number of such moral standards which have been the basis of man's social behavior and which nevertheless have to be recognized. It is not the responsibility of educational psychology to arrive at exact definitions of the form and content of these moral standards. This is the something for social ethics, while the business of psychology is simply to find out whether it is even conceivable to put this into practice in the real world.

Bear in mind that all those revolutionary epochs when the old order breaks down and falls apart often represent such an improbable combination of the most diverse moral cultures that the child may sometimes find it utterly impossible to make any sense of this confusion. Moral crises, therefore, lie in wait for the child at every step of the way, and, consequently, the teacher and educator can in no way ignore questions of moral education. No other epoch creates such magnificent opportunities for moral heroism, and in no other epoch is there such a risk of moral degradation.

Getting accustomed to the spirit of the epoch, to those great currents which permeate the world, is the only criterion here. The purely aesthetic and passive perception of the clarion call of revolution, to which Blok passionately summoned the Russian intelligentsia, writing that, "With all your body, with all your heart, with all your consciousness, heed the call of revolution" – this cannot serve as a foundation of moral education, inasmuch as heeding the call of revolution once upon a time will not lead to active involvement in revolution, and if the poet's summons is to be applied to our actions, it has to so resonate that its meaning express the demand not simply to listen to, but to himself create the music of revolution.

The third basic feature of moral education in our epoch is found in that aspect of truth that distinguishes the ethical outlook which is being created right before our eyes. Truth and the unflinching capacity to face reality squarely in the eye in all the most difficult and all the most confusing circumstances in life – this is the first demand of revolutionary morality. Never before could moral education have reached such an inexorable and absolute truth as now, when absolutely every undisclosed moral "value" has been put on the map and revealed in its true form.

In this as in all other realms, a revolutionary epoch is scarcely able to suggest consummate systems of morality, whatever the previous epochs might have boasted of. Though on the other hand, we may impose on our moral education various individual demands that go well beyond the demands imposed in preceding epochs. We can require that Soviet education train fighters and revolutionaries in the realm of morality, as in all other realms.

We should not set out with the abstract ideal of creating an entire personality, since such a personality does not exist and since such an education would neglect contemporary goals and turn into a game of verbal gymnastics. We confront the concrete goals of training the adults of the next epoch, the adults of the next generation, in full accord with the historical role which will be their lot. Hence the extraordinary degree of specificity and integrity which have become the foundation of moral education in our epoch.

Moral Education Principles

The first question which comes up is to decide on the relationship between moral education and the general education of the personality. In this area, Tolstoy leaned to a negation of all culture, and found that wherever the higher forms of culture flourished, there the higher forms of immorality flourished too. Hence, his conclusions were in the spirit of Rousseau, that the moral ideal lies not in the future, but in the past, that it consists in the negation of civilization and in a return to nature.

That such a view is in radical contradiction to the revolutionary ideology of consciousness of class, an ideology by virtue of which mankind will, in the long run, come to believe in the vigor and dominance of the culturally armed man over nature – this is something no one can deny. There is, however, in Tolstoy's critique of culture an entirely healthy aspect, and this critique may be adopted, though with some corrective, if we take into account the fact that here it is not a matter of culture in general, but of capitalist culture, in particular. There can be no doubt that the moral contradictions reach their zenith at the highest stages of human culture, and that a tribal village represents a healthier moral climate than a European city. But from this one can only conclude that European culture has outlived itself, not that culture in general is antagonistic to morality. On the contrary, since the time of Socrates, the contrary view has been put forward, one which identifies moral behavior with moral consciousness.

"Morality," says Socrates, "is knowledge, and immorality is the fruit of ignorance." Here there is a real psychological problem which is in need of analysis. According to William James "The hackneyed example of moral deliberation is the case of an habitual drunkard under temptation. He has made a resolve to reform, but he is now solicited again by the bottle. His moral triumph or failure literally consists in his finding the right *name* for the case. If he says that it is a case of not wasting good liquor already poured out, or a case of not being churlish and unsociable when in the midst of friends, or a case of learning something at last about a brand of whisky which he never met before, or a case of celebrating a public holiday, or a case of stimulating himself to a more energetic resolve in favor of abstinence than any he has ever yet made, then he is lost; his choice of the wrong name seals his doom.

But if, in spite of all the plausible good names with which his thirsty fancy so copiously furnishes him, he unwaveringly clings to the truer bad name, and apperceives the case as that of 'being a drunkard, being a drunkard, being a drunkard,' his feet are planted on the road to salvation; he saves himself by thinking rightly." Thus, it's as if there was a complete identity established between moral behavior and moral consciousness. "Our moral effort, properly so called, terminates in our holding fast to the appropriate idea. If, then, you are asked, *in what does a moral act consist* when reduced to its simplest and most elementary form? you can make only one reply. You can say that *it consists in the effort of attention by which we hold fast to an idea* which but for that effort of attention would be driven out of the mind by the other psychological tendencies that are there. To *think,* in short, is the secret of will, just as it is the secret of memory".

To find a way out of this awkward situation, we should add that there are facts which at once point to the reverse relationship between consciousness and moral behavior. The reader surely knows that it is one thing to know how to act, and an entirely different thing to act correctly. One can understand perfectly well that alcohol is harmful and nevertheless not have the willpower to give up being an alcoholic.

Obviously, here it is essential to bear in mind that consciousness, of course, plays a kind of role, though not the decisive one, and that it is only one of several components and, quite often, inferior to other, more powerful instinctive drives. Consequently, it is still not enough to provoke the awareness that some good deed is necessary, rather it is far more important to make certain that this idea dominate consciousness, and this means disciplining the child's consciousness so as to assist him in gaining the upper hand over all his conscious and unconscious desires.

Once again, it is not a matter of reducing consciousness to just one thing. In his analysis of the mental state of the alcoholic, James is right to point out that the alcoholic's moral victory or defeat depends wholly on whether he gives the correct name to his state. But one must also ask what this state depends on, and this question, of course, may be answered only in the sense that the very appearance of this or that idea in consciousness depends, in turn, on the different stimuli which have preceded it, and these are usually powerful emotional drives. Consequently, we can speak of conscious influence only when we understand this as something connected with the nervous system, as a system formed by precisely those reactions which all of behavior consists in, though we are speaking only of those reactions which inhibit and regulate the rest of behavior. In other words, only an understanding of consciousness as involving preparatory forms of organization of behavior can supply us with an explanation of the role of consciousness in ensuring proper behavior.

Hence follow several conclusions. There can be no doubt that consciousness exerts a decisive influence on our moral behavior, though there is no direct dependence whatsoever which can be established between the two. It was for this reason that Meumann was able to show that moral development and the general level of education go hand in hand, while Witheft established the rule that success in school has fundamental importance for the student's entire moral existence. The question has to be asked in such a way as to disclose the relationship between success in school and behavior, though this does not mean also explaining this relationship.

Intellectual development may be associated with the greatest immorality, and, consequently, intellectual development, in and of itself, is hardly a guarantee of moral behavior. We also know of the converse, that one may be blessed with luminous moral behavior even though one's intellect is greatly retarded, that retarded children may display a genuinely keen and understanding heart, and, consequently, mental development cannot be taken as even a necessary condition of moral giftedness. Nevertheless, we are still justified in claiming that there exists a profound relationship between the two, and that mental development is a propitious condition for moral education.

Such a relationship denotes a finer life, more complex and more diverse forms of behavior, and, consequently, allows for far greater opportunities and possibilities for educational intervention. In the mentally underdeveloped child, the process of behavior is far simpler and, consequently, there is no opportunity for all those infinitely involved schemes children have to be drawn into in order to influence their behavior.

However, only that form of consciousness proves to be decisive for morality which is directly associated with behavior and realized directly in activity, for otherwise a correct consciousness may lead to incorrect deeds.

All attempts at moral education, at moral sermonizing, must, for these reasons, have to be seen as quite futile. Morality has to constitute an inseparable part of education as a whole at its very roots, and he is acting morally who does not notice that he is acting morally. Just like health, which we notice only when it is disturbed, like the air which we breathe, so does the way we behave in terms of morality arouse in us a whole series of concerns only when there is something seriously wrong with it. Herbart's rule, "not to teach too much," is nowhere as applicable to this extent as in moral education.

It is for this reason that we feel it is pointless to teach morality. Moral precepts, in and of themselves, will, in the student's mind, seem like a collection of purely verbal responses that have absolutely nothing to do with behavior. At its best, such a system is like a motor that has not started up some device and which is doomed to remain idle. At its best, therefore, it may cause some conflict between the child's behavior and the moral precepts. There can be no doubt whatsoever that, for example, the struggle of Tsarist pedagogics against certain childish vices associated with sexual behavior not only did not lead to useful results, but, on the contrary, turned out to have harmful effects, in that it created complex and agonizing feelings in the child's soul.

The child who did not feel capable of dealing with his own desires, who did not know how to counter them, suffered from the consciousness of his own guilt, his own fears, and his own shame, and, as a result, things that were, in and of themselves, not so terrible, were transformed into severe mental and nervous shocks under the influence of such unwise education.

Not only does education in morality seem pointless and harmful, but every form of moral education already seems to attest to a degree of abnormality in this realm. Moral education should be dissolved entirely imperceptibly into all those general modes of behavior that may be established and regulated by the social environment. Neither student nor teacher should think special instruction in morality is called for. Our understanding of moral behavior becomes enlarged, inasmuch as we are then justified in speaking not only of moral behavior in the narrow sense of the term, but also of a moral relationship to things, to oneself, to one's body, and so on.

Moral behavior will always be that which is associated with the free choice of social forms of behavior. Spinoza writes that if a person runs away from something on the grounds that it is bad, he is acting like a slave. Only that person is free, in Spinoza's view, who runs away from something because something else is better. With this as a ground rule, William James gives a perfectly rigorous technique for moral education, on the basis of the principle that one must always proceed not from evil, but from good. "See to it now, I beg you, that you make freemen of your pupils by habituating them to act, whenever possible, under the notion of a good.

Get them habitually to tell the truth, not so much through showing them the wickedness of lying as by arousing their enthusiasm for honor and veracity... And in the lessons which you may be legally obliged to conduct upon the bad effects of alcohol, lay less stress than the books do on the drunkard's stomach, kidneys, nerves, and social miseries, and more on the blessings of having an organism kept in lifelong possession of its full youthful elasticity by a sweet, sound blood, to which stimulants and narcotics are unknown, and to which the morning sun and air and dew will daily come as sufficiently powerful intoxicants".

In other words, we should not proceed in moral education the same way we proceed in thinking of laws in the criminal code, when we refrain from some deed simply because we fear the punishment that would ensue. Do not, in other words, turn morality into the internal policeman of the soul. To avoid something out of fear still does not mean you are performing a good deed.

In this sense, Rousseau was profoundly in error when, wishing to keep his hero Emile away from dangerous and sordid affairs, placed him as a child in a clinic for venereal diseases in the hope that ulcers, stench, shame, and the abasement of the human body would frighten the youth. From the psychological point of view. chastity purchased at the price of fear sullies the soul worse than outright debauchery, inasmuch as it does not destroy all base wishes and desires in the child's mind, but only creates in his mind a petty and mean struggle between these desires and the no less humiliating and no less servile feelings of fear. Only that chastity has any value which is procured by a positive attitude towards action and by an understanding of its true essence. Not to do something out of a fear of dire consequences is just as immoral as to do it. Every unfree attitude towards things, all fear and dependence, already denotes the absence of any moral sensibility. In its psychological sense, the moral is always free.

In this sense, present-day pedagogics is in radical contradiction with religious and, in particular, Christian morality, whose principle tool has been intimidation, threats, and the like. "He whose life is based upon the word 'no,' who tells the truth because a lie is wicked, and who has constantly to grapple with his envious and cowardly and mean propensities, is in an inferior situation in every respect to what he would be if the love of truth and magnanimity positively possessed him from the outset, and he felt no inferior temptations. Your born gentleman is certainly, for this world's purposes, a more valuable being than your 'Crump,' with his grunting resistance to his native devils,' even though in God's sight the latter may, as the Catholic theologians say, be rolling up great stores of 'merit'".

There are three irrefutable drawbacks of this type of pedagogics. First is the fact that it can never be certain of success. It frightens the weak, but arouses resistance in the strong and imparts a special charm of strength, boldness, and challenge to the breaking of rules. It is profoundly remarkable for moral psychology that rebels and those who break the rules of moral psychology are always portrayed in man's imagination in an attractive light simply because they represent strength, unyielding pride, and insubordination to rules. From Byron's passionate heroes to the most commonplace school wit – everything that is insolent and which refuses to surrender to intimidation quite naturally draws the child's sympathies. In such instances, the child seems to respond with the words of the Apostle: "I see what is better and approve of it, but instead I follow what is worse."

The second drawback of this form of moral education, which is always based on the absence of freedom, is that it creates an entirely false picture of moral values, assigning to moral virtue a kind of wealth, arousing self-esteem and a contemptuous attitude towards everything which is wrong. Everyone is forced to experience the sort of agonizing moral conflict that Andreev described in his story, "Darkness," sooner or later, and the time comes for everyone when he recognizes that it is sometimes shameful to be good, just as it is shameful to be rich when it is combined with the terrible darkness of the unenlightened human soul.

And then the honest and morally pure person who has been totally consumed in the enthusiasm to perform good deeds discovers the degradation and insignificance of his own moral purity when confronted by a vulgar prostitute and decides that if we are powerless to illuminate the darkness with our pitiful lanterns, then it is better to extinguish them and start to crawl about on all fours in this darkness.

Finally, the third danger is that every description of misdeeds, by creating a succession of images in the child's mind, creates, at the same time, the impulse and inclination to perform these deeds. Recall that every act of consciousness is a nascent activity, and that, consequently, by cautioning our pupils against what they should not do, we are, at the same time, focusing their attention on these deeds. and thereby encouraging them to perform them. The common expression, that the forbidden fruit is sweetest, contains a great psychological truth, and communicates some of what we have been speaking of here. There is no better way of compelling a child who has picked up a glass to break it than by repeatedly cautioning him. "Now look, don't break it," or "you're going to break it. I'm sure of that." In the same way. there is no surer method of leading a child into carrying out some immoral deed than by describing it in great detail.

This is why Thorndike is quite correct to emphasize the harm brought about by discussing with children in painstaking detail and at great length the motives, methods, and opportunities for committing suicide, as is done in certain French textbooks on morality. To do this means creating in the student's mind propitious conditions and material that might take hold of the child's mind at some point in the future and guide his behavior not away from suicide, but towards it. Explains Thorndike, do not speak to children by telling them, "You must not cut a cat open in order to see what is inside." Every consciousness of some phenomenon contains a certain motor impulse, and this impulse is especially strong in children.

All of us know how much power is exerted over a child's behavior by a book he has just finished reading, in the same way that children who have begun to read James Fenimore Cooper and Captain Mayne-Reade will run off to America to become Indians. Consequently, there is nothing more dangerous in childhood than such teaching of morality, in which, by virtue of natural psychological consequences, the teaching of morality turns into the teaching of immorality. Here we can say, without fear of falling into error, that whereas knowledge of a good deed is far from any guarantee that it will be performed, knowledge of bad deeds will always serve as encouragement.

Moral Transgressions

Every teacher is forced to deal with moral misdeeds

committed by children. These misdeeds may range over an extraordinarily lengthy scale, from slight and insignificant faults to genuine and serious offences, in the form of murder, arson, and so on. Quite analogously, the steps taken by teachers against such children begin with slight and simple verbal reproofs and end in penal colonies for young offenders, where children are kept behind bars and subjected to prison conditions.

How should we view these moral misdeeds in children from the psychological point of view? Until the true nature of morality was discovered, moral behavior seemed to be just as objectively necessary for behavior as are the rules of logic for thinking. Both the adult and the child who has transgressed moral precepts seem to be abnormal, and ill.

In such instances, pedagogics spoke of a moral deficiency in the child, as if speaking of an illness, in the same sense one usually speaks of a mental or physical impairment. It is supposed, moreover, that a moral deficiency is an inborn defect attributable to biological causes, to heredity, or to physiological causes of some defect in the structure of the organism, like congenital blindness or deafness. Thus, it is claimed that there are people who, from the time they are born, are moral and others who, from the time they are born, are immoral, and that, consequently, there are children who, by their very nature, are condemned to sit behind bars, because they are born criminals, just as a blind person is fated never to see light, since he is born without vision.

It goes without saying that, from the point of view of physiology and psychology, such ideas are nonsense. No physiologist has ever had to deal with any sort of special organs of morality in the human body which, if injured, would lead to an absolute love for criminal behavior and for practical jokes. No psychologist in analyzing the forms of human behavior and in explaining the laws governing their development has ever had to confront the existence of such innate reactions that might govern moral or immoral behavior. Thus, the concept of moral imperfection is not a biological concept, but a social concept. It is not innate, but acquired, and arises not from biological factors that guide the development of the organism and its behavior, but from social factors that guide and adapt this behavior to the conditions of existence in the particular environment in which the child has to live.

Thus, moral imperfection always derives from experience and always denotes not a defect in innate reactions and instincts, i.e., not a defect of the organism and of behavior, but a defect of conditional relations for adaptation to the conditions of the environment, i.e., a defect in education. It is, therefore, far more correct to speak not of the moral deficiency of a child, but of his social underdevelopment or neglect. Hence a general conclusion becomes perfectly clear, a conclusion which should serve as a starting point in all questions having to do with the education of such children. These children require no special pedagogics, no protective, corrective, or punitive measures whatsoever, only redoubled social attention and quadrupled educational influence from the direction of the environment.

In every case of moral misdeeds in children, from the least significant on up to the most serious, we are dealing with a conflict between the child and the environment, and we have to recognize that every child is a congenital moral criminal simply by virtue of the fact that he is born with reactions that are notoriously maladjusted to the environment. Even in the utterly most well-educated families, no child is born with the ready ability to behave properly; on the contrary, in absolutely none of his normal actions and deeds does he obey the rules of good breeding and morality, and in this sense the whole task of education is only to help the child adapt to the conditions of his surroundings.

The educational influence of the environment the child is immersed in is the only tool for the adaptation of these reactions. And since under the conditions of the modern order, the social environment is always is always organized in the most discordant way imaginable, consequently, by virtue of the contradictions it contains, there will inevitably always be people in whom anti-social behavioral patterns will consequently evolve simply because they fell under the influence of inauspicious circumstances. Consequently, in these instances we have to think of social re-education as being the only pedagogical tool for overcoming these evils.

Such a child has to be placed in an environment that would foster in him, in place of the anti-social behavioral patterns already established in him, new ways of interacting with people that would also adapt him to the conditions of his existence. A morally imperfect deed is anti-social above all, and moral education is, above all, social education. In this sense, the rule of scientific pedagogics is quite the reverse of what is often employed as regards those who break laws in society and in government. There, banishment from the social environment is the natural thing to do, whereas here, in contrast, the most involved forms of participation, and of social contact, are appropriate.

There, we have an extraordinarily slight concern with the character of the offender himself, and all our concern is directed towards rendering him harmless and safeguarding the environment from his influence. Here, in contrast, our concern must be directed towards preserving and transforming the child's character and, consequently, our goal is the most thoroughgoing re-education of the child. Nowadays, even the state in its punitive policies has begun to assume that point of view towards offenders which views punishment as being intended to serve the purposes of reeducation rather than of intimidation and retribution. And just as in the case of serious offences, so does the slightest misdeed committed by a child ultimately always point to a greater or lesser schism in the child's social behavior.

Therefore, like criminal behavior generally, criminal behavior in children does not at all point to a low overall development of the individual. On the contrary, an offence points often to a certain strength, the capacity to rebel, considerable freedom, and the capacity for powerful feelings – and the capacity to desire much and to achieve much.

Under the conditions of bourgeois morality and truth, everything that exceeds the bounds of the average man is banished to become the province of criminals, of those who sense a force in themselves and who cannot be reconciled with the established way of life. Dostoyevskil, in speaking of his novel, *The House of the Dead,* remarked that in the prisons for hard labor, one could find the most gifted, the most forceful members of the populace gathered there, except for the fact those forces had been corrupted, perverted, and employed for evil purposes.

Similarly, childhood offenses not only do not indicate any sort of defect in the child's psyche, but, on the contrary, are bound up with and are quite compatible with considerable overall giftedness. Moral offenses not only do not point to an inability in the child for the acquisition of social skills or his incapacity for social relationships, on the contrary, very often such a child will exhibit an extraordinary degree of guile, cunning, ingenuity, true heroism, and, what is most important, the greatest devotion to a special morality of his own, whether of street thieves or pickpockets, who have their own morality, their own professional ethics, their own concept of good and evil.

More often than not, this moral imbalance in a child springs from two fundamental causes. First, there is homelessness, which constitutes a fact of enormous social significance and, in its true sense, is comparable to the absence of all social education, i.e., all concern for the development of adaptive reactions to the environment. On the other hand, there is the problem of children who, though highly gifted, cannot find any outlet for their energy in ordinary patterns of behavior.

On the contrary, in terms of morality, obedient children usually represent a vivid example of ungiftedness, simply because they tend very often to suffer from rickets or are anemic or are dull and narrow-minded, follow the line of easiest adaptation to the environment, and either do not need very much, or who, very early in childhood, grasped the secret of a happy life and value it above all other blessings. People with great passions, people who accomplish great deeds, people who possess strong feelings, even people with great minds and a strong personality, rarely come out of good little boys and girls.

There is no one feature of the traditional moral education that attests so eloquently against this system as do these instances. In other words, not only in those instances when moral education has not succeeded, but far more often in those instances when it has succeeded, does moral education reveal its utter impotence. Nowhere has it achieved such degradation as where it achieved everything it wished. It is here that its true nature stands revealed. We have seen that wherever it did not succeed, it testified to its own utter impotence, creating, in theory, a concept of congenital moral deficiency, and, in practice, replacing desks in school by bars in prison and the school routine by forced labor conditions, entrusting prison wardens with the responsibility of completing those duties that teachers had left incomplete.

But this also happened whenever it experienced the triumph of its own force and power, wherever it reaped total success, even where it discovered it was capable only of creating a loyal and cautious child, one who was faint-hearted and inclined to be obedient, timid, and dutiful. This occurred simply because the whole system of moral education was constructed on authoritarian principles, i.e., with the recognition of that special compulsory value of the authority of parents and teachers, which sustained the sanctions of punishments and rewards, deterrence and happiness. "Listen to your elders, and you'll be good, otherwise you'll be bad" – such is the inelegant, though exact formula of this form of pedagogics.

The higher moral value was recognized in an obedience that was motivated by fear, whereas, from the psychological point of view, obedience itself lacks all power of moral instruction, inasmuch as it supposes in advance an unfree and servile attitude towards things and towards deeds. Thus, the fundamental psychological mechanism that served as the foundation of moral education was, in fact, the most profound pedagogical delusion imaginable.

It is extraordinarily important to note in this regard that this mechanism has penetrated so deeply into our flesh and blood that even the most progressive teacher and the most well-educated parent is unable to free himself of this timeworn technique, and when a mother tells her child, "Don't do this, else Mama won't love you," she is making the very same mistake, except in gentler form, as the police do when they put a very young thief behind bars. A child can, in fact, abstain from his misdeeds, but the moral and educational influence of his abstention will either be null, or can even be negative, inasmuch as it is purchased at the price of fear, at the price of humiliation, and not at the price of the child's true rebirth. This is why obedience is, for us, of negligible moral value, and the good behavior purchased at the price of obedience is not, in our eyes, a pedagogical ideal.

All the same, the authoritarian principle in morality from which this authority must have emanated in one way or another must be demolished, and in its place something entirely new must be erected. The closest we can get to a definition of this new principle, which is to become the foundation of moral education, is to view it from general approaches to education, as consisting in the social coordination of one's own behavior with the behavior of the group, and here obedience must be replaced throughout by free social coordination.

The rule that originates from everyone, from the group, and which is directed likewise to the entire group and sustained by the actual effective mechanism of the self-discipline and routine of daily life in the school has to itself replace that "pedagogical singsong" which prevails between teacher and student in the authoritarian system.

It is not obedience to someone or obedience to something, but the free adoption of those patterns of behavior which will vouchsafe the consonance of all of behavior. This mechanism is not something alien to the child, something that grips him, on the contrary, it lies within the child's very nature, and play is the natural mechanism which develops and connects these skills together. Nowhere is the child's behavior so regulated by rules as in play, and nowhere does it assume such a free and morally instructive form as in play. Nowhere in play do we find any patterns whatsoever that an adult might have prescribed and which the child only enact.

On the contrary, games are the natural seedlings of future moral behavior. The child obeys the rules of a game not because he is threatened with punishment or, on the other hand, because he is scared of failing in something or of losing something, but only because observing the rules – which is a promise that he renews from one minute to the next – vouchsafes him the inner satisfaction that comes from playing a game, because here he acts as part of the general enterprise that is formed out of a group at play. Breaking a rule does not represent any threat. whatsoever other than the fact that, at that moment, the game has not worked out, and the child has lost interest in it, and this is a powerful enough incentive for regulating the child's behavior.

Accordingly, it is clear what steps have to be taken by the teacher to counter the various moral transgressions a child may commit. In the authoritarian system of morality, every moral rule was accompanied by a particular sanction which entailed punishing the child in the event of disobedience, and awarding him when he obeyed. Punishment and rewards assumed the most diverse forms, from corporeal punishment, being sent to bed without supper, or being locked up in a jail cell, and all the various kinds of rewards right up through rather fine and delicate forms, for example, reprimands, censure, and, in the case of rewards, praise. The pedagogical utility, or, more properly, the harm produced by these measures was extremely variable, though they all served as tools for producing commonplace, unthinking reactions and, in the best case, taught only the virtue of obedience, only the single moral rule – avoidance of what is unpleasant.

And if we were to imagine that this sanction were lifted and the child could imagine that his misdeeds would produce not the slightest reaction on the part of those around him, he would not have the slightest reason to refrain from engaging in these deeds. Moral behavior must be based not on external prohibition, but on internal restraint, even more properly, on the fact that man is naturally drawn to the good and the beautiful. Moral behavior must become the individual's true nature and be enacted freely and effortlessly.

The idea that the child's own will is his best teacher is still very much alive in pedagogics. There is the view held by many instructors which teaches not to protect children from danger, but to let them experience the unhealthy consequences of their own deeds as if in an experiment, and to learn to avoid them on their own. Thus, if a child is in the habit of instinctively reaching out to a lit candle or to a hot samovar, it is the opinion of these teachers that he should not be kept from doing so.

On the contrary, he should be given the opportunity to bum himself, that this is the best school for the child, it is this which teaches him to beware of fire better than any other measure. In the very psychological mechanism of pain and the striving to avoid it, teachers have found a mighty tool, and the example just presented represents a typical instance of such an education.

In critically examining this approach, we have to bear in mind that, when applied to instances of this type, in which a healthy effect is associated directly with some deed, this type of educational measure could hardly become widespread and assume the status of a general principle. How should a teacher proceed if he wishes to act in accordance with this rule and allow children to have the experience of the adverse consequences of their deeds, and how should he proceed when the adverse consequence of some deed does not manifest itself immediately, but only after a prolonged period of time, or only after many years? Isn't it true that, after all this time, the child could end up becoming accustomed to bad habits, and that all the harm he finds out about afterwards will not be able to save him from it? The harmful consequences of a single cigarette may be negligible and, in fact, imperceptible, but if we allow the child to, in fact, experience the harm of smoking, we run the risk of fostering in him an experienced smoker long before he comes to the realization that he has to renounce the very idea of being a smoker.

Instances in which harmful consequences are associated with just such a connection with some deed are just as likely, which makes the relationship between this deed and its adverse consequences difficult and incomprehensible to the child's understanding. Finally, there are a whole series of deeds that induce such destructive consequences as to make it extremely risky to trust in their educational influence. If a child has a yearning to jump out the window, a teacher would hardly think it reasonable to allow him to do so in order to actually learn the harmful consequences that this would bring about. There is an extraordinarily large number of such instances, with effects that not only involve physical harm, but also moral harm.

Thus, the application of this principle could be limited to insignificant cases of the type presented above, but it cannot be of general pedagogical value, and, in particular, it is entirely inappropriate for the education of moral behavior. It lacks that essential freedom of choice which alone is capable of leading to moral behavior. Natorp says somewhere that we don't in the least think that people without jobs could turn into angels if they were to be given their freedom. We only know that they become devils when they feel they are being oppressed. And in the same sense, it seems entirely clear and self evident that this principle of pain is not appropriate for justifying punishment. The child learns very quickly to understand that punishment is not at all necessarily related to his misdeeds, but that there is an additional and intermediate component here expressed in the intervention of adults, and he learns to avoid this intervention, to conceal his deeds, to tell lies, and so on.

Besides, every form of punishment places both the teacher and the student in the most painful and difficult of positions. Neither love nor respect nor trust can be preserved between a teacher who is inflicting punishment and the child he is punishing. Every form of punishment, no matter what it involves, always places the student in a humiliating position, and undermines his love and trust. Herbart says in this regard that, "Threats are a poor educational tool; they tempt strong natures and are of little effect in keeping weak natures away from misdeeds, because they do not have the power to combat their negative desires. Desires make mincemeat of the fear of punishment."

In other words, every form of punishment is harmful, from the psychological point of view, and there is no place whatsoever for punishment in Soviet schools. The very idea of a child committing some misdeed always points to a defect in the educational process. An offense committed by a student is, above all, an offense committed by the school, and only the elimination of this defect in the social organization of the school itself is appropriate. In this sense, self-governance in the school and the self-discipline of the children themselves are the best tools for moral education in the school.

One must take care that the forms assumed by such self-governance not turn into a mere replica of adult behavioral patterns, and that interest in artificial formalities does not kill the vital sense of community in the child. Accordingly, organizing the social environment in the school is not simply a matter of creating a constitution of school governance and of summoning children to general assemblies at regular intervals of time, of making choices and maintaining all those forms of communal organization that children are so eager to copy from adults.

Rather, it means concern for those genuinely social relations that have to permeate this environment. Beginning with intimate and friendly relations that reach down to the smallest social groups, then moving on to the broadest associations of comrades, and ending in the broadest and largest forms of children's movements, the school has to penetrate and envelop the life of the child with a myriad of social relations that could assist in the development of moral character. In no other realm does the general thesis of education – that to educate means to impart a discipline to life, and in a properly conducted life, it means to raise children properly – possess as much force and validity as here.

Hence, the relation between education and life, and between the school and the social order, becomes understandable, moreover that this relation must serve as a starting point for pedagogics. Questions of education will be fully solved only when questions of social order have been fully solved. Every attempt at constructing educational ideals in a society with social contradictions is a utopian dream, since, as we have seen, the social environment is the only educational factor that can establish new reactions in the child, and so long as it harbors unresolved contradictions, these contradictions will create cracks in the most well thought-out and most inspired educational system.

Accordingly, in the present transitional epoch we will always have to deal with undesirable patterns of behavior in children, and, before anything else, we have to be ready to deal with the complex and difficult work of re-education. Next we have to find out how to retain the positive aspects of the system of rewards and punishment as educational measures for Soviet pedagogics.

Though rewards and punishments have to be banished from Soviet schools because of their harmful influence, it is nevertheless beyond question that some portion of their effect will have to be retained, for otherwise the nature of children's drives, which happen to be a powerful motivation of their deeds, will have to be made use of in the realm of moral education. This positive element should be retained, and manifest itself through the reversion, or return, of every one of a child's actions back to him in the form of the impressions of the effect it has on those around him. Nothing so arouses us to act as the satisfaction associated with it.

This is the reason why William James was able to discern a positive element in the system of grades, and even insisted that children be told their grades. It is here that James discovered a realization of that psychological law according to which, through the work cycle, our own deed reverts back to us, in the form of a reflected impression. "We thus receive sensible news of our behavior and its results. We hear the words we have spoken, feel our own blow as we give it, or read in the bystander's eyes the success or failure of our conduct. Now this return wave of impression pertains to the completeness of the whole experience But so far as our psychological deduction goes, it would suggest that the pupil's eagerness to know how well he does is in the line of his normal completeness of function, and should never be baulked except for very definite reasons indeed.

Acquaint them, therefore, with their marks and standing and prospects, unless in the individual case you have some special practical reason for not so doing."

We have not presented these thoughts of William James not in order to make a defense of the grading systems used in public schools. On the contrary, that grading systems are psychologically inappropriate is entirely self-evident from the reasoning presented above in our discussion of punishment.

A grade is a form of assessment so alien to the entire course of school work that it very quickly starts to dominate the natural concerns of teaching, and the student begins to learn for the sake of avoiding bad grades or for the sake of obtaining good grades. Similarly, grades combine all the negative aspects of praise and censure. There is in these remarks of his a great psychological truth, however, that the child should always know the ultimate results of his own deeds, and that this knowledge is a powerful educational tool in the hands of the teacher.

Therefore, a public school should not be understood as simply consisting in a crowd of children who have nothing to do with one other. We all know that bringing together any large group of children who have nothing to do with one other and who do not share any common interests makes each child feel his isolation and loneliness even more acutely. Nowhere does a person feel so alone as when he is in a crowd he has no connection to or when he is in a modern capitalist city, where no one has any feelings for or understanding of another person. Such a system is capable only of stifling the child, and has a profoundly oppressive effect upon him. Obviously, in the Soviet school we have to be concerned with those forms of public education that would induce vital interaction between children so that the child would place a high value on the satisfaction or dissatisfaction of his classmates. With these social structures in place, the environment becomes a powerful mechanism that is forever conveying to the child the reflected impression of his own actions.

In a properly ordered social environment, the child will always think of himself as fully transparent, as if reflected by a vast resonator, and all those reflected impressions of his own deeds he will be discovering all the time will become the most powerful educational tool in the hands of the teacher.

It is thus not hard to see that the child's relationship to his surroundings will not in the least always bear that propitious and idyllic character in which "free" education pictures itself.

The ideals of free education, i.e., the absolutely uninhibited pursuit of the child's deeds, arouses objections from two points of view. First, it is almost never possible to actually realize free education in its entirety, and, consequently, we are always left with only a pedagogical principle possessing a certain degree of relative force within quite narrow limits. The child's desires will always encompass much that is destructive and harmful, and, left to his own devices, a child could cause himself so much harm that no teacher in his right mind would be opposed to discouraging a child from undertaking this or that deed in the name of the principles of free education.

Moreover, complete freedom in education means rejecting all forethought and all social adaptation, i.e., in other words, all educational influence. But, education denotes a restriction and restraint of freedom from the very outset. To the extent that education is an unavoidable process in man's life, to that extent free education denotes not a rejection of constraints in general, rather it means imparting to those constraints the elemental force of the situation in which the child lives. If a person refuses education proper, he begins to be educated by furniture, by the street, and by things in general.

Thus, free education must be understood exclusively as denoting education which is as free as it can be within the constraints of an overall educational program and within the constraints of the social environment. Thus may it always turn out, and, in fact, it often turns out that the child's behavior is far from the same thing as the interests of the group. Then conflict may always arise, which, without forcing the child to do anything in particular, will make him see the value of changing the way he behaves so as to accord with the interests of the group. The school routine should be so organized that the child finds it best to go in step with the group, in the same way as when he is at play; that any departure from the group seem just as meaningless as quitting a game. Just like playing a game, life should demand a constant straining at the leash, a constant joy in concerted activity.

Ultimately, the theory of free education is the other side of the theory of innateness of moral sensibility. Both concede that pedagogical intervention is powerless and of no use in the development and growth of the child, and both suppose that what is most important in the child's moral response is already present at birth. Thus do both come to the conclusion quite naturally that there are children who are good and children who are bad, children who are moral and children who are immoral, from the moment they are born and in their very nature.

In the belief that "moral degradation is inherited," Gaupp presented in confirmation of this thesis testimony given by parents who, in speaking of their own child, declared that "[he] *could not be normal*; he is altogether different from other children; from the very beginning he was not the same as other children; he possessed an ineradicable desire to do evil."

Tolstoy, likewise, supposes that the child possesses an ineradicable drive to do good. There is the very same mistake being made here; faith in the innateness of moral behavior and a lack of understanding of the fact that moral behavior is wholly the product of education.

Bibliography

Bjorklund, D.F. & Pellegrini, A.D., Child Development and Evolutionary Psychology. Child Development, 2000.

Chandler, P. & Sweller, J.., "Cognitive Load Theory and the Format of Instruction," Cognition and Instruction 8 (4): 293-332, 1991.

Clark, R.C., Mayer, R.E., e-Learning and the Science of Instruction: Proven Guidelines for Consumers and Designers of Multimedia Learning, San Francisco: Pfeiffer, 2002.

Cooper, G., & Sweller, J., "Effects of schema acquisition and rule automation on mathematical problem-solving transfer," Journal of Educational Psychology 79 (4): 1987.

Geary, D. C., & Bjorklund, D. F., Evolutionary developmental psychology, Child Development, 71, 2000.

Johnson-Pynn, J., Fragaszy, D.M., & Cummins-Sebree, S., Common territories in comparative and developmental psychology: The quest for shared means and meaning in behavioral investigations. International Journal of Comparative Psychology, 2003.

MacDonald, K., & Hershberger, S., Theoretical Issues in the Study of Evolution and Development, In R. Burgess and K. MacDonald (Eds.), Evolutionary Perspectives on Human Development, 2nd edition,. Thousand Oaks, CA: Sage, 2005.

Mayer, R.E., Bove,W. Bryman, A. Mars,R. & Tapangco, L., "When Less Is More: Meaningful Learning From Visual and Verbal Summaries of Science Textbook Lessons," Journal of Educational Psychology. 88 (1): 64-73, 1996.

Rich Gibson, The Frozen Dialectics of Paulo Freire, in *NeoLiberalism and Education Reform,* Hampton Press, 2006.

Sweller, J., & Cooper, G. A., "The use of worked examples as a substitute for problem solving in learning algebra", Cognition and Instruction 2 (1): 59-89, 1985.

Sweller, J., "Cognitive load during problem solving: Effects on learning", Cognitive Science 12 (1): 257-285, 1988.

Theodora Polito, Educational Theory as Theory of Culture: A Vichian perspective on the educational theories of John Dewey and Kieran Egan Educational Philosophy and Theory, 2005.

Index